NEW DIRECTIONS IN THEATRE

General Editor JULIAN HILTON

NEW DIRECTIONS IN THEATRE

Published titles

Forthcoming titles

Theatre as Action

Soviet Russian Avant-Garde Aesthetics

LARS KLEBERG

Translated from Swedish by Charles Rougle

First published in Swedish 1980 by
Bokförlaget PAN/Norstedts
Stockholm

First published in English 1993 by
THE MACMILLAN PRESS LTD
Houndmills, Basingstoke, Hampshire RG21 2XS
and London
Companies and representatives
throughout the world

ISBN 0–333–56694–7 hardcover
ISBN 0–333–56817–6 paperback

A catalogue record for this book is available
from the British Library

Printed in Hong Kong

Contents

General Editor's Preface

In the past ten years, Theatre Studies has experienced remarkable international growth, students seeing in its marriage of the practical and the intellectual a creative and rewarding discipline. Some countries are now opening school and degree programmes in Theatre Studies for the first time; others are having to accommodate to the fact that a popular subject attracting large numbers of highly motivated students has to be given greater attention than hitherto. The professional theatre itself is changing, as graduates of degree and diploma programmes make their way through the 'fringe' into established theatre companies, film and television.

Two changes in attitudes have occurred as a result: first, that the relationship between teachers and practitioners has significantly improved, not least because many more people now have experience of both; secondly, that the widespread academic suspicion about theatre as a subject for study has at least been squarely faced, if not fully discredited. Yet there is still much to be done to translate the practical and educational achievements of the past decade into coherent theory, and this series is intended as a contribution to that task. Its contributors are chosen for their combination of professional and didactic skills, and are drawn from a wide range of countries, languages and styles in order to give some impression of the subject in its international perspective.

This series offers no single programme or ideology; yet all its authors have in common the sense of being in a period of transition and debate out of which the theory and practice of theatre cannot but emerge in a new form.

JULIAN HILTON

vii

Preface

In the debates on 'revolutionary art' or 'cultural revolution' in the 1920s in Soviet Russia, several discourses seem to be intertwined, to run parallel, and even, at times, to coincide. The same can be said of the concept of the homogeneous and 'representative' auditorium during the period of theatrical modernism. One of the primary tasks of the analysis in the present book has been to distinguish and contrast different concepts, even at points where they sometimes seem to be using the same words. This has called for a somewhat archaeological approach of reconstruction and conjecture. Contemporaries of the period in question perhaps found it easier to distinguish between positions which at a historical distance tend to be swallowed up in a single '1920s discourse'. For example, the avant-gardists, the Proletkult activists, and the few Bolsheviks interested in art were in reality associated with quite different cultural contexts which automatically guaranteed various decodings of their sometimes almost identical phraseology. The reader of today is necessarily obliged to adopt an approach that reactivates these contexts and sharpens such distinctions.

If distinguishing and differentiating is the first of the two basic strategies of this study, the second seems to lead in the opposite direction. For the sake of conclusive comparisons, the analysis sometimes simplifies, and sometimes deliberately overexposes phenomena of rather different levels (for example, the theatrical practice of naturalist staging and the utopian programme of 'ritual theatre'). In retrospect, some of these typological strictures may appear somewhat 'anatomical', but because they are essential to the composition of the book, I have chosen to leave them largely unaltered from the original version.

In revising the text for the English edition I have generally tried to avoid superficially 'updating' the frame of reference; my afterthoughts are to be found in the Postscript. Certain passages have been shortened, some new paragraphs added, and the chapter 'The Provisional Abdication of Total Theatre' is new. The bibliographic references have been thoroughly revised with a view to the English-speaking reader. Apart from these changes, the central arguments of the book stand as they were formulated fifteen years ago.

Re-reading the original 1977 Swedish edition of the book, I have noted (with mixed feelings of satisfaction and disappointment) that the wealth of research on the Russian avant-garde and the Soviet 1920s published in the meantime has not rendered my treatment of the basic issue obsolete: the interrelationship between art and the public, or, in the language of semiotics, the pragmatic aspect of art. Furthermore, what must be considered the new standard work in the field, Konstantin Rudnitsky's strictly inductive survey *Russian and Soviet Theatre. Tradition and the Avant-Garde* (1988) seems to lend support both to the typology proposed here and to my strong emphasis on the Wagnerian heritage and the popular mixture of symbolism and communism, aspects which in 1977 were not commonly treated either in Soviet or in Western scholarship.

The reservations the book may raise in retrospect probably have to do with its limited scope. The focus on the politicised segment of the avant-garde viewed as the centre of Russian cultural life was obviously the choice of a sympathiser – a sympathiser, however, who was more interested in analysing the crisis of the movement than in proposing an uncritical reception of it. Thus the book was and still is not an attempt to write the history of the Soviet Russian theatre of the 1920s. Its composition is determined by the theme: the self-reflection of a political avant-garde art situated, roughly speaking, in a field delimited by the names of Vsevolod Meyerhold and Bertolt Brecht. The choice of both subject and method has obvious roots in the perspective of the 1970s, but this is not the only reason my book is out of tune with the current 'about-face' trend in Soviet cultural history, which proposes a general inversion of former established hierarchies and proportions and sometimes ends in little more than a new hagiography: instead of Mayakovsky – Mandelstam; instead of Meyerhold – Tairov; instead of Lenin – Berdyayev; and so on. My aim was and is not to contribute to such new hierarchy-building. If there is today a specific context to which the study of the 1920s transformations of certain avant-garde myths relates, it is probably that of the post-modernist debate.

*   *   *

In the preface to the first edition of this book I quoted the Swedish critic Ulf Linde, who remarked: 'What you are not able to translate, you haven't really understood.'

My friend Charles Rougle's translation of the text is based on a true understanding of the subject, and has certainly provoked me to clarify or revise a number of points. For different reasons – one of them being the geographical distance that now separates us – we have not been able to finish work on the book in the close collaboration in which it was begun.

Nevertheless, I want to thank Professor Rougle for his painstaking labours, which – once again – have helped a Swedish scholarly work appear in an English that is clearer and more intelligible than its original version, perhaps, deserves.

Also, I would like to thank Dr Richard Taylor of the University College of Swansea for reading the penultimate version of the manuscript and for providing valuable comments before it was delivered to the careful editors of Macmillan. I am especially indebted to Professor Julian Hilton, general editor of the New Directions in Theatre series, for his inspiring comments and patient support during the revision of the book. Any remaining flaws or obscurities, of course, are entirely my responsibility.

Special research for chapter 9 has been made possible by a short-term grant from the Kennan Institute of Advanced Russian studies in Washington, DC.

The translation of the book has been made possible by a grant from the Swedish Council for Research in the Humanities and Social Sciences, which is hereby gratefully acknowledged.

Moscow – Funbo,
August 1991

L. K.

Part I

Avant-Garde Art and the Project of Cultural Revolution

Chapter 1

Iconoclasm and Festival

Sergey Eisenstein's film *October* (1928) opens with a shot from the street below of a gigantic statue of Tsar Alexander III silhouetted in imperturbable majesty against the sky. Suddenly, however, ladders are propped against the statue, people scramble up them, and, like Lilliputians swarming over a dead cast-iron Gulliver, begin wrapping ropes around the figure of the tsar. The lines are drawn taut, and finally this ponderous idol of the autocracy comes crashing to the ground. The February Revolution of 1917 has arrived.[1]

The immobile statue toppled by the rebellious masses is the leitmotif that runs through Eisenstein's extraordinarily deliberately structured film from the first frame to the last. Other monuments in 'petrified' Petrograd are also associated with the hollow statue of Alexander, and they are joined by the Winter Palace's fetish world of methodically arranged porcelain, weapons, servants, and ultimately by the entire old regime whose symbols of power the Provisional Government vainly attempts to keep aloft. When the evening of 25 October – the date of the Bolshevik takeover – arrives, Prime Minister Kerensky has already fled. The remnants of the government sit petrified and wait for the end; finally, when the masses storm the Winter Palace, only their empty fur coats are left.

Starkly contrasted with the dead, hollow world of fetishes in Eisenstein's film are the living, throbbing crowds on the streets and in the squares, in the countryside and at the front, at the Congress of Soviets and outside the Winter Palace. The spontaneous energy of the people is increasingly organised and disciplined by Lenin and the Bolsheviks as

2

the moment of revolt approaches. When the signal is given, this energy explodes, and the crowd rushes furiously across Palace Square and storms the Winter Palace. The pent-up hatred of generations gushes forth in a veritable rape of the already impotent symbol of oppression and exploitation as the wine cellar is plundered, furniture is overturned, and the endless staircases and corridors are soiled for the first time by the heavy shoes and felt boots of the common people. The clocks show 00.00. A new age has begun.

The opposition 'dead idols' versus 'rebellious masses' that Eisenstein develops metaphorically throughout the film can be considered archetypal. The destruction of the bronze or marble images of the tyrants has been an almost obligatory element in political rebellion from long before our era to Budapest in 1956, Saigon in 1975, and Russia in 1991. It is part of the 'festival of the suppressed and exploited', as Lenin in a moment of rhetorical enthusiasm once referred to the Revolution.

If iconoclasm is the symbolic act of the revolt itself, that of the victorious revolution is the mass fête that commemorates the day of the revolt and confirms that the revolution is still alive. In modern times before 1917 there are examples of this during both the French Revolution just after 1789 and the Paris Commune in 1871. On 14 July 1791, Jacques Louis David, who was not only the great painter of the Revolution but also the organiser of festivities for the National Convention, mobilised the citizens to celebrate the anniversary of the storming of the Bastille. The masses paraded through Paris and gathered around a huge bonfire, where they burned attributes of the monarchy and released thousands of doves carrying Declarations of Freedom. This and similar festivals became the models for later mass spectacles in France and during the Civil War in Soviet Russia.[2] For obvious reasons, the Paris Commune staged no commemorative festivals during the 72 days of its existence, but it did arrange the legendary removal of the Vendôme Column that the dictator Napoleon Bonaparte had raised to eternalise his colonial victories.

The controversies over the cultural revolution in early Soviet Russia can be approached in the examples of *monumental sculpture* and *the theatre*, the most public of all art forms. The debates of the revolutionary artistic intelligentsia about iconoclasm and especially about theatre with and for the people, which is the main theme of the present study, bring to the fore a number of vital questions about culture and revolution, including the utility value of the cultural heritage and of contemporary art, and the relationship between artist, work and audience.

The new Russian poetry, theatre and art before the Revolution had broken radically with the conventions of nineteenth-century realism and had issued to bourgeois society its declaration of independence. The symbolist poetry, enigmatic theatrical mysteries and ornamental paint- ing that emerged around the turn of the century no longer offered any routine 'common sense' picture of reality – that task was now left to popular literature, the press and the cinema. Art was thereby liberated from its traditional functions of representing the official ideology of the state or of satisfying the demands of new social strata for mirror images of their lives and dreams. This *autonomy*, this sovereign freedom that art enjoyed from 'everyday' demands, however, was dearly purchased: it entailed isolation both from the public at large and from the raw materi- als of experience that had previously provided a bond between artist and audience. The struggle for emancipation ended in the Ivory Tower.

Certain writers and artists made a virtue of the inescapable fact of isolation. They shunned the despicable 'crowd' and declared that the lost ability of art to address anything but itself was a true victory. On the whole, however, the notion of 'art for art's sake' never really took root in Russia, where art and literature had almost always been approached from an ethical (religious or social) perspective. After the abortive 1905 Revolution symbolist poets began to stress the collective and socially therapeutic mission of art in general and of the theatre in particular. The fervour of their utopian programmes was intensified by the fact that their contact with the public had been undermined by the double-edged pro- cess of autonomisation.

Among those who in Russia pushed art's abandonment of its tradi- tional mimetic and ideological functions to the limit were futurist poets such as Velimir Khlebnikov and Vladimir Mayakovsky, and artists such as Vladimir Tatlin and Kazimir Malevich. Poetry, the futurists declared, should work with the pure relationship between sound and meaning, with 'the word as such'. Our pictures are constructions, said the non- figurative artists; we do not portray reality but create new objects. With a great hullabaloo the avant-gardists attacked the conservative art estab- lishment and delivered 'a slap in the face of public taste', to cite the title of one famous futurist manifesto.

When the spokesmen for the avant-garde movement declared earlier art to be dead and demanded that the classics Pushkin, Dostoevsky and Tolstoy be 'thrown overboard from the Steamship of Modernity', they were being deliberately provocative in order to attract attention and to enlist the support of those spectators who wanted to avoid being num- bered among the Philistines.[3] But the avant-garde also had a bold positive programme that aimed at bringing art out of the isolation of special auditoriums, museums and libraries and on to the streets and squares. If art was no longer the depiction and description of reality but *the creation of new things*, then there was no longer any essential difference between 'art' and 'life'. Art as a specially insulated and regulated restricted area was abolished, and painters, poets, theatre directors, and so on were given infinite scope to fill reality with novel beautiful forms and sensations, even to shape everyday reality itself according to the principles of the new beauty. The avant-garde artists, it is true, regarded themselves as being as high above the man on the street as their predecessors had done, but now they were no longer romantic prophets or naturalistic reporters but 'moulders of life'.[4]

Thus may be summarised the avant-garde's attack on the 'institution of art' in Russia during the hectic years prior to the October Revolution. It was not, of course, anything specifically Russian, as similar violent leaps from the isolation of the Ivory Tower to 'the abolition of art' were also proclaimed by West European futurists and dadaists. One should emphasise the word *proclaimed*, for abolishing the closed work of art and dissolving art in everyday life was, and largely remained, little more than a utopian dream.

The Russian avant-garde's first heroic attacks on the bastions of bourgeois art took place on the eve of the First World War. While the establishment let it be known that it had no intention of being abolished, it opened the door a crack to the aggressive 'attackers', who soon began to become more or less established themselves. Soon after the Revolution, however, the avant-garde rallied fresh troops in the hope of accomplishing a third upheaval, now in the realm of art, to follow the political and social revolutions of February and October 1917. Never before had the utopian dream of abolishing the institution of art and transforming everyday reality into a gigantic spectacle, a pulsating and glittering *Gesamtkunstwerk*, seemed so near to realisation. What was to follow, however, was instead a period of intense ideological struggle in the area of art and culture that forced the avant-garde to revise its positions and reformulate or completely abandon the utopia. Using primarily the theatre as illustration, the present study is an attempt to describe that process.

Eisenstein's tenth-anniversary film *October* was in many ways a balance sheet of a period that was fast becoming history and legend. When revolutionary political action was no longer possible in reality, it became instead a theme in art. The same was true of the avant-garde's utopian projects: the dream of abolishing the work of art and erasing the boundary between life and theatre – symbolised by the razing of the

Decree No. 1 on the Democratisation of the Arts

(wall literature and market-place painting)

Comrades and citizens, we, the leaders of futurism – the revolutionary art of youth – hereby declare:

1. Henceforth, with the destruction of the tsarist order, the presence of art in the storerooms and barns of human genius – palaces, galleries, salons, libraries, theatres – is *cancelled*.

2. That in the name of the great stride toward the equality of all before culture, the *Free Word* of the creative individual be written on the corners of the houses, on fences, roofs and streets of our cities and villages, on the backs of automobiles, carriages, streetcars and on the clothing of all citizens.

3. That *paintings* (colours) be cast like brilliant rainbows over the streets and squares from building to building to delight and ennoble the eye (taste) of the passer-by.

Artists and writers are obliged immediately to take their paint-pots and with the brushes of their skills illuminate, decorate all the sides, foreheads and breasts of the cities, railway stations, and ever rushing flocks of railroad cars.

Henceforth, as he goes along the street, may the citizen each minute savour the profound thought of his great contemporaries, contemplate the brilliance of the beautiful joy of Today, listen to the music – the melodies, roar, noise – of wonderful composers everywhere.

Let the streets be a holiday of art for all.

And if it turns out as we say, all who go out upon the street will be elevated and made wiser as they contemplate the beauty that has replaced the streets of today – iron books (signs) in which page after page is filled only by the letters of greed, acquisitiveness, egoistic meanness and base stupidity that sullies the soul and insults the eye. 'All art to all the people!'

The first poems will be pasted up and pictures will be hung in Moscow the day our paper is published.

V. Mayakovsky, V. Kamensky, D. Burlyuk

From *The Futurist Newspaper*, No. 1 (1918)

statue and by the mass spectacle – are here encapsulated in a work of art which for all its technical radicalism was produced and consumed in accordance with traditional norms.

The time for cultural revolution was by now definitely past. Ten years after 1917 an official myth of the Revolution was in the making, and art was rehearsing the rôle in which it had been cast by the Stalinist society that was under construction.[5]

Chapter 2

The Project of Cultural Revolution

In search of a cultural policy

When the Bolsheviks seized power in October 1917 they had no theory describing the rôle culture and the entire superstructure would play in the future socialist society. Leading Marxist theorists and critics such as Mehring and Plekhanov had developed general ideas on the function of culture in bourgeois and feudal society, and in this area they had made important contributions. The concrete questions of cultural policy that interested the parties of the Second International, however, were for the most part limited to education and cultural propagation within the labour movement under capitalism. Scarcely any thought at all had been given to the question of the *active participatory rôle* culture and ideology would play, once the working class had accomplished the socialist revolution and embarked upon what Marxist theory declared to be its historic mission of abolishing class society.

The Bolsheviks' ambition to take over and revolutionise politics and existing institutions after October 25 was no easier to realise in culture than elsewhere. If anything, it was more difficult. Commissar of Enlightenment Anatoly Lunacharsky was no Lenin or Trotsky but a broadminded and far from doctrinaire socialist with little experience of practical politics. Critics within his own party and his opponents among the intelligentsia often sarcastically, and on one occasion appreciatively, referred to him as 'soft-hearted Anatoly'.

The shortcomings of Narkompros (the Russian acronym for the Commissariat of Enlightenment), its vacillation between different points of view and its inability to execute decisions, however, did not derive solely from Lunacharsky's personal weaknesses or sympathies. His and Narkompros's efforts were grandiose and ambitious, but they were inhibited on the one hand by the economic crisis and the initially almost total boycott of the cultural intelligentsia, and on the other by the absence within the Party and government of a coherent theory that could serve to guide cultural policy.[1]

With characteristic candour, Lunacharsky was the first to admit the lack of a theory for cultural policy in general and for a policy on the arts in particular. Looking back over the experience of the first years he declared in 1923:

> The questions of state policy on the arts are not easy to handle. Our efforts in the area have on numerous occasions been affected by the abrupt zig-zag manoeuvres that the transition to the New Economic Policy has forced the Soviet state to execute. As to what constitutes Marxist aesthetics, the ideology of art from a Marxist viewpoint, that question has just recently been raised and has received little consideration. Our mentors have hardly even touched upon these questions, and we have far from established an orthodox Marxist view of art.[2]

Just how far from 'an orthodox Marxist view of art' Lunacharsky himself stood or at least was prepared to move for tactical reasons is apparent from his appeal to the cultural workers of Petrograd in November 1917. He describes the coup a couple of weeks earlier as a purely 'popular', democratic revolution that has abolished 'the boundaries of class and caste' at a single blow:

> The end has come not only for the autocratic and bureaucratic regime that has inhibited art, but also for every manner of class and caste prejudice. We must create new, free and purely popular forms of artistic life.
>
> Within this important area of cultural work the working people need your help, and you will give them that help.[3]

The vast majority of cultural figures rebuffed all of 'soft-hearted Anatoly's' invitations to cooperate with the revolutionary government. According to Mayakovsky's account ten years later, among those who designed to respond at all the prevailing view was similar to that of

Fyodor Sologub, who had said that revolutions should be banned from urban centres with many cultural treasures such as Petersburg and conducted outside the city limits; only when all the fighting was over should the revolutionaries be allowed to march back in.[4]

At first, only a handful of cultural workers responded favourably to the Soviet government's appeals for cooperation. The legendary meeting at the Smolny, to which all the writers and artists of Petrograd had been invited but which only Mayakovsky, Blok, Meyerhold and a couple of others attended, must be considered part of revolutionary mythology (the earliest testimony about this much cited meeting is dated 1935, and no documents have yet been found that can prove that it ever took place!). Still, the legend of the valiant five or six does contain a symbolic truth.[5]

Eventually Lunacharsky managed to attract to Narkompros certain representatives of the pre-revolutionary cultural establishment whose patriotism and concern for cultural treasures outweighed their doubts as to the Bolsheviks' legitimacy. Among these were not only artist and art critic Alexander Benois and Yuzhin-Sumbatov and Nemirovich-Danchenko from the 'academic' theatres, but also writers such as Alexander Blok and Maxim Gorky. For these men, who represented the right wing of Narkompros, defence of the cultural heritage and philanthropic cultural enlightenment were heartfelt concerns. To his left Lunacharsky had two groups whose cultural revolutionary ambitions soon proved mutually incompatible: Proletkult and the artistic avant-garde led by the futurists.

Culture as collective creativity: the Proletkult

The Proletkult (the Russian acronym for 'Proletarian cultural-educational organisation') was a peculiar mass movement that played an important but controversial rôle during the first years of the Soviet regime. Only recently has scholarly research done full justice to its historical significance.[6] The Proletkult movement was founded on the eve of the October Revolution. Its ideological platform was strongly influenced by the socialist theoretician Alexander Bogdanov, who had been Lenin's only rival for leadership of the Bolshevik Party during its early years. With its elaborate programme, subsidies from Narkompros, and mass membership, Proletkult became a significant socio-cultural force in the new state.

In contrast to the Bolshevik leaders, Proletkult had already before the October Revolution developed a relatively articulate theory about the rôle culture in the broadest sense should play under socialism in general and in particular during the dictatorship of the proletariat that was to usher in the classless society.

In the factional struggles that followed the abortive 1905 Revolution, alongside the Bolsheviks around Lenin there had crystallised a group of disillusioned Social Democrat intellectuals who considered that any successful social revolution must be prepared for by a cultural revolution. This rather heterogeneous group included such subsequently well known figures as Anatoly Lunacharsky, Maxim Gorky, Alexandra Kollontai and, in the centre as the leading theoretician and organiser, Alexander Bogdanov.

As early as 1910, when the revolution in Russia had been suppressed and the labour movement was in the midst of a profound crisis, Bogdanov had advanced his notion of 'proletarian culture' as a prerequisite for the future leading rôle of the working class. The collectivistic proletarian ideology that had arisen under capitalism, he said, was itself a step toward the future:

> And yet socialism is not only the future but also the present, not only theory but also reality. It is growing and developing, it is already among us, although not where our opportunistic comrades are looking for it. It is the comradely solidarity of the working class; it is its conscious organisation in work and in the social struggle.[7]

'Opportunistic comrades' refers to Lenin and his group, with whom Bogdanov had broken off relations over what he considered to be meaningless or even harmful participation in government-controlled parliamentary politics (the Third Duma). A new, proletarian culture was to insulate the working class from the ideology and institutions of bourgeois society and, through self-education, help it instead to prepare for its historical mission.

As a philosopher Bogdanov to some extent erased the traditional Marxian opposition of base and superstructure through an overarching concept of *organisation* borrowed from the natural rather than the social sciences. Like many other contemporary thinkers, he subscribed to the 'monistic' view that the fundamental unity of the world extended to both culture and nature. Bogdanov's view of reality in general and the working class in particular was marked by evolutionism, collectivism and radical utopianism. At the core of his theory was not the class struggle but the organisation of the collective through the ever-widening circles of the production process. In this peculiar synthesis of scientific theory,

Marxism, and Nietzschean visions of the superman, the working class represented the (thus far) highest stage of human evolution.

As early as 1908, Lenin had attempted to disarm Bogdanov politically by labelling him a 'philosophical idealist'. Bogdanov, however, who had been the foremost Bolshevik spokesman at the 1907 Social Democratic Congress in London, continued to exert a strong influence on émigré socialist intellectuals. He remained, to cite the title of the first monograph on his life and work, 'Lenin's rival'.

On 16–17 October 1917, the first conference of the cultural-educational organisations of Petrograd was convened on the initiative of the Petrograd factory committees. Among the leaders of the new organisations, which would soon spread across the Russian Republic under the name Proletkult, were a number of Bogdanov's closest supporters from the years of emigration: Anatoly Lunacharsky (married to Bogdanov's sister), Fyodor Kalinin and Pavel Lebedev-Polyansky. The resolution adopted by the conference noted that the organisation was autonomous *vis-à-vis* the Bolshevik Party, the trade unions and the cooperatives; that its function was to 'arm the working class with knowledge and organise its emotions with the help of art'; and that the proletariat would proceed on the basis of previous culture to develop its 'independent creative activity' within both science and art.

The proletarian cultural organisation led by Bogdanov's followers was thus already in existence before the October Revolution. For that reason and by virtue of Lunacharsky's double rôle, Proletkult was in a strong position relative to Narkompros. During the first six months of 1918, it had access to state subsidies totalling some 9 million rubles, which can be compared with the 32 million that went to adult education and about 16 million to higher education.[8] Basing its argument on the principle that organisation of the working class involved three equal areas, however, Proletkult consistently stressed its independence of the state and the Bolshevik Party. What the Party was in *politics* and the trade unions in the *economic* struggle, Proletkult would be in the *cultural* sphere. This principle was set forth as early as the October conference, thus before the Bolshevik takeover, and it was destined to arouse violent controversy during the next few years.

Proletkult's central concept was the 'collective creation' or synthesis of ideology and material production whose class character by definition placed it on a higher level than earlier cultural forms. From this followed a rigorous vigilance against influence from other classes or strata, especially the petty bourgeois intelligentsia. In artistic work – which according to the resolution adopted by the first All-Russian Proletkult

The Proletariat and Art

A resolution presented by Alexander Bogdanov at the First All-Russian Conference of Proletarian cultural and educational organisations.

1. Through living images, art organises social experience not only in the sphere of knowledge, but also in the sphere of emotions and aspirations. This makes it the mightiest tool for the organisation of collective forces, and in a class society, for the organisation of class forces.

2. In order to organise its forces in societal work, struggle and construction, the proletariat must have its own class art. The spirit of this art is labour collectivism: it perceives and reflects the world from the point of view of the labour collective, expresses the link between its emotions and its will to struggle and create.

3. The treasures of the old art must not be assimilated passively, for in that case they would educate the working class in the spirit of the culture of the ruling classes and thereby in a spirit of subordination to the order of life created by these classes. The proletariat must approach the treasures of the old art critically, with a new interpretation that reveals their hidden collective foundations and their organisational meaning. If this is done, they will become a valuable heritage for the proletariat, a weapon in its struggle against the old world that created them, and a tool in the organisation of the new world. The transmission of this artistic heritage is a task for the proletarian critics.

4. All organisations, all institutions devoting themselves to the development of the new art and the new criticism, should be organised on the principle of comradely collaboration, which directly cultivates the socialist ideal.

Adopted unanimously, one abstaining.
20 September 1918

From *Proletarian Culture*, No. 5 (1918)

---

conference in September 1918 was 'the mightiest tool for organising the powers of the collective' – this attitude implied considerable confidence in collectively organised creation. Against the study of the cultural forms of bourgeois society and professionalism in general, priority was given to 'proletarian spontaneity', which was to guarantee purity and genuineness of expression. One of Proletkult's theatrical studios declared in early 1919:

> The socialist theatre should be founded on the ambition to allow the proletariat to develop artistically and in full its collective 'I' in theatrical creation. The workers' dramatic studio is a free studio. Here there will be no lessons in 'acting', but only in developing and correcting the individuality of the worker actors so that they may preserve that immediacy of proletarian spirit that is the necessary prerequisite for the creation of the collective's own theatre.[9]

This peculiar spontaneity assumed that the workers who came to the Proletkult studios were blank pages. In reality, of course, they were influenced in art as elsewhere by their social experience. Usually, therefore, it was imitations of familiar models – pre-symbolist poetry, stylised art nouveau painting, etc. – that became the 'spontaneous' mould in which Proletkult's young worker artists cast the 'spontaneous' ideology of the proletarian superman which Bogdanov's followers had developed and propagated for them.

The professional cultural revolution: the avant-garde

The Artists' Union in Petrograd, which was independent of the government, had been actively working since May 1917 to gain control of institutions such as the Academy of Arts. The Union maintained that it had the right of 'self-determination' *vis-à-vis* the Provisional Government and, after October, *vis-à-vis* the Soviet state. Lunacharsky dismissed such ambitions as 'syndicalist', and in April 1918 Narkompros closed the Academy of Arts. The task of reorganising it was given not to the official candidate of the Artists' Union but to a representative of its 'left' wing, Nikolay Punin. This gave the avant-garde a foothold within Narkompros, where until 1920 they exerted considerable influence especially in IZO, the visual arts section. The newspaper *Iskusstvo Kommuny* (*Art of the Commune*), to which among others Mayakovsky, Osip Brik, Kazimir Malevich and Punin were regular contributors, became IZO's press organ during its publication between December 1918 and April 1919.

Within Narkompros and in the public debate of 1918–19 the avant-garde advanced a radical programme of cultural revolution for the arts policy of the Soviet state. Whereas Proletkult was a mass movement with an established ideological line and an organisation that paralleled that of the Bolsheviks or the trade unions, the avant-garde was a limited group of individuals who shared above all a professional interest in cultural policy.[10]

The avant-garde programme was developed in a two-front war against the 'academic' art establishment, on the one hand, and Proletkult's mass movement, on the other. The struggle had two aspects. In the vacuum that arose after the Revolution, when the majority of the cultural intelligentsia turned their backs on the Soviet government and the state itself lacked theoretical guidelines for a cultural policy, the avant-garde – or 'left art', as it was often referred to – was given an unique opportunity to realise its projects *through the state*. Punin declared in so many words that 'futurism is state art' and that the dictatorship of the (avant-garde) minority was the only correct line in arts policy:

> We want to see our October Revolution realised; we want to assert the dictatorship of the minority, for the minority is the only creative group with muscles strong enough to keep up with the working class.[11]

When the 'academics' and Proletkult acquired influence and financial support in different areas within Narkompros, the left reacted with jealous insinuations that their rivals were after the economic resources of the new state patron of the arts. Probably the only effect of such accusations was to cast doubt on the unselfishness of the avant-garde's own ambitions for power.

The question of access to power and subsidies is only one side of the avant-garde's struggle in 1918–19. The other and more interesting one is the restatement of the problem of art as ideology versus art as material production that was presented in *Art of the Commune's* polemics with Proletkult.

The core of Proletkult's programme for cultural revolution was to liberate the spontaneous ideology of the 'new' class. Exactly contrary to this was the avant-garde's theory of culture, which maintained that the most important prerequisite for the creation of art was not feeling but skill. Futurism especially had developed a new type of work of art that was less and less representational and more and more an autonomous 'thing'. The textbook example, of course, is the collage, a combination of materials on a plane surface that does not *represent* any three-dimensional space but *is* an object in space. Not just any object, however. By departing from the practice of both professionals and amateurs since time immemorial and creating new *things* rather than images, the avant-garde artist seemed finally to have broken out of the ideological sphere and into material production as a technical specialist or design engineer.

Osip Brik was perhaps the first to articulate theoretically this view of the artist as producer and to integrate it into the discussion about the proletariat, culture and the Revolution. A series of his articles in *Art of the Commune* in 1918–19 outlined the main features in the 'production aesthetics' that a few years later would acquire great significance in the Soviet Union and which have indirectly influenced the Western European artistic debate in recent years. In the most significant of his articles, 'The Proletarian Artist', Brik made an attempt to abolish the well known opposition between 'art for the proletariat' and 'art by the proletariat' by speaking instead of 'art by proletarian artists' or 'artist-proletarians'. Anyone, he said, would agree that art in the new society was going to be 'proletarian art'. But this unanimity was only superficial. Who was to create this art? 'Art for the proletariat' was merely an attempt to transfer the passive bourgeois 'appreciation of art' to the socialist society by extending the sphere of influence of traditional art to include the working class. Here the polemical edge cuts at Lunacharsky's and especially Lenin's position on cultural policy, which was above all to break the bourgeois monopoly on education.

What, then, of 'art *by* the proletariat', which was Proletkult's programme for spontaneous creation? That, said Brik, was merely a poor antithesis of bourgeois art. The cult of genius and commercialism were simply exchanged for a worship of spontaneity that would not result in any authentic proletarian creation but only in 'a wretched parody of the long obsolete forms of the old art'.

Art is production, Brik declared. The professional, technically accomplished artist participates in social production and is therefore a proletarian among others: 'The proletarian artist unites two things: creative talent and proletarian consciousness'.[12]

The opposition between 'art for the workers' and 'art by the workers', on the one hand, and art as labour, on the other, can be viewed from a non-normative and sociological perspective. The point, as Brik wrote in another context, is not how art *should* develop, but how it *will* develop.

Thus reformulated, the relationship between art and the new society had the advantage of resulting not in a utopia, like Proletkult's programme, but in a prognosis. At the same time, however, Brik's discussion of the surrounding society was based on a notion that had very little to do with the reality of the Soviet Russia of 1918. Yet his political

Osip Brik
The Proletarian Artist

The art of the future is proletarian art. Art will either be proletarian or it will not be at all.

But who will create it?

Those who by proletarian art mean 'art for the proletariat' answer immediately that this art, like all other art, will be created by artistic 'talents'. According to them, talent is something universal. It can easily be adapted to any consumer. Today the bourgeoisie, tomorrow the proletarian – what's the difference? These persons, who cannot rid themselves of the bourgeois consumerist attitude, want to give the proletariat the completely alien role of a patron on a mass scale that graciously allows himself to be amused by entertaining tricks. Hence the constant concern for 'intelligibility', 'accessibility', as if this were the main thing. It is an old well-known fact that the more intelligible and accessible art is, the more boring it is. But the 'talents' are terrified of irritating their new consumers with something surprising and daring, and prefer to force feed them with murderous boredom.

The art of the future will not be created by them. These soulless artisans, these petty bourgeois who have nothing in common with the living revolutionary proletarian consciousness, are doomed to destruction together with the bourgeois forces that gave birth to them.

'The proletarians themselves', reply those who by proletarian art mean 'art by the proletariat'. They think that it is enough to take any proletarian whatever and give him an education and all he produces will be proletarian art. Experience has shown, however, that instead of proletarian creation the result is a wretched parody of the long-exhausted forms of the old art. And this cannot be otherwise, for art does not tolerate amateurism any better than any other production. This fact Proletkult has forgotten.

Proletarian art is not 'art for the proletariat' and not 'art by the proletariat', but art by proletarian artists. They and only they will create this new art of the future.

The proletarian artist unites two things: a creative talent and proletarian consciousness. And they have not been joined temporarily, just for a time, but have fused into an indivisible whole.

The proletarian artist differs from the bourgeois artist not because he is creating for another consumer, and not because he comes from a different social environment, but by virtue of his relationship to himself and his art.

The bourgeois artist regarded creation as his private affair; the proletarian artist knows that he and his talent belong to the collective.

The bourgeois artist created to assert his own personality; the proletarian artist creates to perform a socially significant task.

The bourgeois artist separated himself from the masses as an element that was alien to him; the proletarian artist sees before him his equals.

In his quest for fame and fortune, the bourgeois artist strove to adapt himself to the taste of the masses; the proletarian artist, who knows no personal profit, combats the inertia of the masses and leads them along the paths of art that is constantly forging ahead.

The bourgeois artist repeats thousands of time the clichés of the past; the proletarian artist always creates something new, for therein is his social mission.

These are the fundamental principles of proletarian creation. He who acknowledges them is a proletarian, a proletarian artist, a builder of the art of the future.

From *Art of the Commune*, No. 2 (1918)

---

illusions were shared by many: in addition to his colleagues at *Art of the Commune*, there was Proletkult and, in Party politics, the 'left Communists' in 1918–19 and the Workers' Opposition a couple of years later. The fact of the matter was that, while Proletkult was talking about developing pure proletarian culture and the avant-garde was speaking of art in the technological society, Russia was entering a civil war that threatened to destroy the entire production apparatus and eliminate the working class.

The crisis of 1920–1921 and the defeat of the maximalists

It was of course no coincidence that the offensive of the Bolshevik Party leaders against the left in Narkompros, Proletkult and the artistic avant-garde ran parallel to the crisis within the Party at the end of the Civil War (between the Ninth and Tenth Party Congresses in March–April 1920 and March 1921, respectively). We shall not attempt here to provide any complete historical picture of this period, but merely juxtapose certain simultaneously occurring events in the cultural and political spheres.

Upon the conclusion of the Civil War in the spring of 1921, Lenin introduced his so-called New Economic Policy (NEP), explaining its implications in his tract 'On the Tax in Kind' (April 1921). Although the truths laid down in the article were apparently self-evident, they were at that moment salt in the wound of the left opposition in the Party and various opposition groups outside it. For the vast majority of the population, however, NEP meant at least a partial return to 'normal', that is pre-revolutionary, relations.

As Lenin had pointed out to the left opposition as early as 1918–19, the dictatorship of the proletariat did not imply that socialism had been achieved, or even could be achieved for some time. According to Lenin, there were in fact five different competing socio-economic formations in the Soviet state: patriarchal peasant farming (natural economy); small commodity production (peasants who sold their grain); private capitalism; state capitalism; socialism. The left opposition sometimes sounded as if they believed that 'War Communism' was at least the path to socialism, if indeed socialism had not already arrived. Lenin in 1921 meant something quite different – it was an illusion to think that the Soviet state was anything but a transitional society dominated by small-scale capitalism.

In Lenin's view, the reality of 1920–1 demanded a compromise with capitalism, and this made NEP a vital necessity. Statistics on the situation in the country spoke for themselves. Of a population of 136 million, the proletariat represented only 4.6 million, of which 2 million could be considered industrial workers (the figures in 1913 were 11 and 3 million respectively). One-tenth of this proletariat, about 500,000, were members of the Bolshevik Party. Approximately 80 per cent of the population were peasants. Nearly 70 per cent of the country was illiterate. Average industrial production in 1920–1 had sunk to 15–20 per cent of the 1913 level. Food rations in the cities were at half the subsistence level – the rest had to be obtained on the black market. If one adds to this familiar statistical picture the fact presented at the Fourth Congress of Trade Unions that an average worker in the spring of 1920 had to spend two and a half to three times his wages on the barest necessities, the strikes and peasant revolts of 1920 and early 1921 are not surprising. The Kronstadt revolt in March 1921 was the climax of a series of such events.[13]

What is surprising, however, is that the left-wing maximalists could under such circumstances regard the compromise with small-scale capitalism and the peasants as a betrayal of the proletariat. When, at a meeting discussing trade union policy, Lenin said something that would seem self-evident, namely that 'we do not really have a workers' state, but a workers' and peasants' state', Bukharin, one of the top Party leaders, shouted in a very irritated tone of voice: 'What kind of state? A workers' and *peasants'* state?'[14]

Bukharin was still opposed to any compromise with the peasants – or with reality, if you will – and continued to use the rhetoric of War Communism. The strikes and peasant revolts, however, spoke a different language, pointing instead to an acute economic crisis that at any moment could become political. At the same time, between the Ninth and Tenth Party Congresses the Bolsheviks were split by violent inner strife that could only be suppressed by the 'temporary' ban on factions adopted at the latter. The remarkable fact is that almost all oppositional voices within the Party and the trade unions came from the *left* and shared Bukharin's blindness to the overall balance of forces in the country. The Workers' Opposition – which was the largest group attacking the revision of War Communism – criticised above all suppression of the workers' initiative at the factories in favour of management by directors and experts. As one of the leaders, Alexandra Kollontay, declared in her pamphlet *The Workers' Opposition*: 'Only workers can generate in their mind new methods of organising labour as well as running industry.'[15]

Phrasing and concepts in *The Workers' Opposition* such as class purity, spontaneous proletarian consciousness, organisation, and so on, bring to mind Bogdanov and Proletkult. Although Kollontay had known Bogdanov since the pre-war emigration years, she did not belong to Proletkult. However, no organisational link between Proletkult and the Workers' Opposition was needed to arouse Lenin's misgivings. To him, the most serious thing about Proletkult was that its sectarian ideology had a mass base beyond Party control in an organisation led by his old rival. Both Lenin's enormous effort to discredit Bogdanov as a philosopher in the Party struggle of 1908 (although not before or after that date) and, beginning in August 1920, his sudden interest in Proletkult's organisation and connection with Narkompros were primarily politically motivated. Even if Proletkult's figures for 1920 of 500,000 participants and 80,000 actual members were exaggerated, it is clear that the organisation provided at least a potential mass base for a maximalist political offensive against NEP. Originally founded on the initiative of the syndicalist-minded factory committees and with acknowledged influence in the trade unions, Proletkult had solid workplace support from both Bolsheviks and especially non-Party workers, a group to which the Party would soon be paying considerable attention. Beginning in the autumn of 1921, Proletkult was in effect forbidden to start new clubs at factories and enterprises. This occurred two days before the Second All-Russian Proletkult Congress, where an anonymous brochure entitled *We Collectivists* was disseminated. Its authors expressed solidarity with Bogdanov and admitted their membership in the Workers' Opposition that had been outlawed at the Tenth Party Congress.[16]

Its network of contacts at workplaces destroyed and its membership and state subsidies dwindling, Proletkult was forced to abandon mass-scale work and to retreat to professional training activities in the studio. One typical if extreme example of this evolution was Proletkult's First Workers' Theatre in Moscow.

The shifts in cultural policy that followed the introduction of NEP in 1921 put the competing revolutionary groups on the defensive. In response to the new situation, the avant-garde, which had been entirely removed from the leadership of all cultural bodies, and parts of the Proletkult movement, which had been forced out of the workplace and strangled economically by a reorganised Narkompros, rallied around a new revolutionary cultural programme – so-called *production art*.

'Lenin's view of culture'

The considerable body of literature that has been published in the Soviet Union about Lenin and questions of art and culture can give the impression that the Bolshevik leader had an elaborate and original cultural theory that for decades has evoked constant interest (and almost no disagreement). The canonical Soviet collection *V. I. Lenin on Literature and Art*, the seventh edition of which appeared in 1986, is 526 pages long. Very few of the texts included, however, specifically address the relationship between art and culture and socialist society. Most of what has been written on Lenin and culture, therefore, must be regarded as pure reconstructions of views ascribed to the creator of Soviet Marxism.

We shall not go into the history of these reconstructions here, but it is worth noting that no systematic 'Lenin's views on culture' were formulated until long after the Bolshevik leader's death in 1924. Only when the doctrine of Socialist Realism was being elaborated were the previously ignored articles 'Party Organisation and Party Literature' (1905) and 'Tolstoy as a Mirror of the Russian Revolution' (1908) raised from polemical texts to Gospel utterances on literature.

The Bolshevik leader who showed the most interest in and insight into literature and art was Leo Trotsky. He wrote a series of brilliant if arrogantly phrased articles on the different trends in Russian literature after the revolution which were collected in 1923 in the book *Literature and Revolution*. He held a negative, not to say derisive attitude toward the monopolistic claim of both futurist and proletarian writers to represent the only authentic model of culture for the new society. According to Trotsky, the creation of a separate proletarian culture – as well as a 'proletarian science' – was false in theory and useless in practice. The task of the proletariat was great enough: it was to abolish class society, and to succeed in this undertaking what was needed first of all was quite simply more education (it was projected that the eradication of illiteracy would take a decade). Although he obviously held these views very early on, Trotsky (probably because he was occupied with other matters he considered more urgent) did not participate in any of the public polemics on the cultural revolution.[17]

Lenin himself, however, did formulate certain views on culture in socialist society in a series of articles on the various 'infantile diseases' of communism in 1918–21. His most quoted statements were made in the autumn of 1920, that is, just before the change of course to NEP was declared. At the Third Congress of the Communist Youth League on 2 October, Lenin listed the most important cultural tasks facing the Soviet state: to crush the upper classes' monopoly on education, primarily by eradicating illiteracy; to 'critically absorb' the cultural heritage of the old society; having critically assessed the entire cultural heritage, to move forward and create a socialist (not 'proletarian') culture based on a Marxist interpretation of the experience of the new society.

One week later, on 9 October, Lenin and the Central Committee of the Party foisted upon the First All-Russian Proletkult Congress in Moscow a resolution that marked the beginning of the end of the movement. Delegates to the congress were forced to condemn both the programme for pure proletarian art and the related demand for organisational autonomy *vis-à-vis* the state.

Lenin's criticism of Proletkult differed significantly from that levelled by avant-gardists such as Brik. Unlike these, he singled out a feature the two revolutionary groups had in common: both believed that the illiterate masses could and should proceed directly from the church (the culture they *really* possessed) to 'spontaneous creation' or to an appreciation of non-figurative art without making a 'detour' through the culture of bourgeois society.[18]

Production art

In his *On New Systems in Art* (1919) Malevich declared that: 'Cubism and futurism were revolutionary movements in art anticipating the revolution in the economic and political life of *1917*.' The idea of experimental art as the harbinger of social upheaval is not new. What has been called 'the myth of the two avant-gardes' is part of the modernist tradition and can be traced back to the French utopian socialists Saint-Simon and Fourier. When the political revolution became reality in Russia in 1917, the 'myth' was revitalised, and the avant-gardists had occasion to repeat Malevich's remark many times during the coming years.[19]

Even a quick glance at what was going on beyond Russia's borders, of course, reveals that cubism and futurism as universal phenomena far from reliably signalled social revolutions in Europe. Probably the most striking connection between art and society here is rather that the fascination with technology and industry typical of many Russian and Italian avant-gardists was in *inverse* proportion to the low level of the productive forces in the two countries. In other words, the less advanced the scale of production, the more fervent the cult of technology and urbanism, the bolder the projects for fusing art and production.

If Malevich's thesis on the prognostic or even pioneering role of art in relation to economy and politics has no theoretical value, it is still of interest to a study of avant-garde art. Here, however, we must make a distinction. Although the avant-garde's own efforts in manifestos and other statements to generalise, explain and legitimise their experiences are often referred to as 'theories', such expressions of self-reflection, which at times assume the form of an entire coherent 'myth', should more properly be called *doctrines*. The avant-garde's own doctrines, unsuitable as analytical models, are instead themselves an important part of the object to be investigated. The interesting point about Malevich's thesis from that perspective is that it expresses the avant-garde view of art not as a passive, retrospective 'reflection', but as an autonomous part of production in the broadest sense.

The most consistent formulation of art as production was presented by Osip Brik in *Art of the Commune*. Although Brik was a brilliant critic, however, he tended to leave the detailed elaboration of his ideas to others. In this case, it was Boris Arvatov who undertook the further development of the theory. Arvatov belonged to Proletkult, publishing his first article, a rather traditional essay on the Doric column in Greek architecture, in its journal *Gorn* (*The Forge*) in 1919. The subject might seem surprising in a journal that took 'Proletarians in all countries, unite!' as its motto, but in fact it was quite characteristic. As we shall see below, Nietzschean worship of Greek antiquity and the relationship of art to ritual were very topical themes to the ideologists of 'pure proletarian creation'. By the time Arvatov published again, in Proletkult's theoretical organ *Proletarskaya kultura* (*Proletarian Culture*) in early 1920, he had evidently gone through Osip Brik's hard school, for now he presented a broad review of the development of art from the sociological perspective of 'production theory' and capped it with a visionary programme for the new art.

Futurism and the latest developments in the visual arts had previously been categorically dismissed, especially by Proletkult's leading ideologists, as 'reflections of the decay of bourgeois society', 'expressions of a reactionary, moribund ideology', and so on. Arvatov proposed instead that all art, especially that of the avant-garde, be regarded as a technological rather than an ideological manifestation. If the history of art is viewed against the background of the conflict between technological progress and capitalist property relations, Arvatov said, we can see how art has abandoned its original utilitarian (cognitive) function and become an increasingly isolated sphere of its own, an illusory retreat from reality (still lifes, non-figurative painting). The revolution, however, signified a radical change in relations of production. Collective worker ownership of the factories would enable the artist once again to play a meaningful social rôle:

> This creates the conditions for completely free creation by all in their chosen fields, without any external coercion. This creative activity will at the same time be a creation of life itself, since the technology through which inspiration bears its fruit is contemporary production engineering. The proletarian artist will transform his work into a vitally necessary function, and art will become a form of skilled labour.[20]

Arvatov's ecstatic vision of the union of the 'proletarian artist' with industrial labour – it rather resembles a collective fête – clearly demonstrates how the technological utopia seems to become more extreme the less actually functioning industry the society in question possesses.[21]

The theory of production art had two sides, one of which was analytic, the other programmatic. Arvatov's 1920 and later analyses of art as a part of social production and of art as a commodity are original for their time in that they leave ideological criticism behind and concentrate on the sociological aspects of art. When he then proceeded to draft a programme for art in the future society, however, he took a prodigious leap from analysis to utopia. This was nothing unique to Arvatov. On the contrary, it was quite typical of the Soviet cultural revolutionaries who, in a country with 100 million peasants and 2 million industrial workers, an almost paralysed production apparatus and trade largely conducted on the black market, nevertheless drafted plans for a communist society in which necessities were no longer commodities and the distinction between manual and intellectual labour had been abolished. For many, the implicit or explicit postulate that *utopia is here* served to legitimise the continued autonomy of artistic experiment, only under the protection of a new patron. For others, the awakening and reorientation in actual NEP class society was a long and troublesome experience.

Arvatov's article in *Proletarian Culture* was not just a casual essay. During the spring of 1920 he gave several lectures at the Moscow Proletkult in which he argued for the theory of production art as a platform upon which the increasingly hard pressed revolutionary currents in culture could collaborate.

The theory of production art soon acquired a base at InKhuK (the Institute of Artistic Culture), an art school founded in Moscow in May 1920. The first programme of the Institute was drafted by Vasily Kandinsky, but after a heated debate it was rejected, and by the end of the year 'production art' had become the prevailing line. Brik and Arvatov were regular lecturers and debaters there. Soon Malevich and his pupils also left the Institute, which thus became totally dominated by leading representatives of the new 'utilitarian aesthetics' such as Alexander Rodchenko and Varvara Stepanova. InKhuK became a laboratory of *constructivist* aesthetics, which advocated transferring the material and composition techniques of non-figurative art to various areas of industrial production. It was proposed that artists should enlist in factories as technical experts to apply their skills. Avant-garde utopianism – art as the 'moulding of life' – seemed to have been suddenly supplanted by pure utilitarianism. As so often before, it was Osip Brik who stated the issue in the most categorical terms:

> We maintain that architects, sculptors and painters are just as much workers as are engineers and workers in the metal, textile or wood industries, and that there is no reason to distinguish their labour as 'creative' from other, 'non-creative' labour.[22]

Even in its most ascetically utilitarian form, however, the theory of production art was *an aesthetics of the producer* that proceeded 'from

form to function'; that is, formal solutions were ascribed a utilitarian
function. But what was there to guarantee that one form was more useful
than another? In the theatre, where the producer was almost tangibly
confronted by the consumer, or spectator, this question became acute.

If utility was indeed the focus of the production artists, then one
would think that all available means, including traditional mimetic devices, should have been equally acceptable. In practice, however, a
distinction was drawn between a 'maximum' and a 'minimum' programme: on the one hand, experiments with art as 'things', constructions, prototypes, and on the other, agitation, satire, emotional impact.
This dualistic division recurs again and again under different names in
the discussion of political avant-garde art during the following years, but
it was a static distinction that could not be developed. It was not until the
centre of gravity shifted from the *producer* viewed as a solitary subject
to the *relationship* between producer and audience, and thus to the
question of how art exerted its influence, that the old opposition between
form and content (which underlay the division into minimum and maximum programmes) could be reformulated. Such a shift, and the subsequent discussions on the ideal versus real rôle of the audience, could
only take place in the latter half of the 1920s. In 1929 Mayakovsky made
the following statement:

> All of our differences with opponents and friends as to whether the
> 'how' or the 'what' of writing is the more important are now resolved
> by the literary slogan *'for what'* to write; that is, we assert *the primacy
> of the end over both form and content.*[23]

The path leading to that view was anything but self-evident for the
avant-garde, whose experiments from the outset addressed problems of
production more than those of reception.

Chapter 3

Down with the Fetishes!

The modern cult of the statue

The classical custom of portraying both mythological figures and leaders of state in marble was revived in Europe during the Renaissance. It was not until bourgeois society matured in the nineteenth century, however, that it became common to immortalise in neo-classical form not only military leaders and monarchs by the Grace of God, but also scientists, artists and finally even the 'heroes' of enterprise and local politics.[1]

Marinetti's remark in the first Italian Futurist manifesto (1909) that a speeding racing car is more beautiful than the ancient Nike of Samothrace was soon to become a well-known cliché. In his 1912 'Technical Manifesto of Futurist Sculpture' the artist Umberto Boccioni developed a more detailed critique of the pseudo-classical 'cult of the statue' and introduced the principles of the new three-dimensional art. Although painting continues to advance in the age of speed and technology, Boccioni stated, sculpture continues to linger on imitations of classical and Renaissance figures. The new, futuristic sculpture renounces all mimetic ambitions and is predicated instead on the internal laws of spatial construction. It is based on 'those wonderful mathematical and geometrical elements of which objects are composed in our own times' and includes movement as a central principle. The isolation of sculpture from the surrounding environment will in this way be broken:

[its basis] will be architectural, not only as a construction of masses, but in such a way that the sculptural block itself will contain the

architectural elements of the *sculptural environment* in which the
object exists.

In this way we will be producing a sculpture of the *environment*.[2]

In the writings of the Russian futurists in general and Mayakovsky in
particular, statues – immobile expressions of bodies in motion, dead
images of living beings – became a recurrent polemical and poetic motif.
When the futurists proclaimed in their manifesto 'Slap in the Face of
Public Taste' that Pushkin, Dostoevsky, Tolstoy et al. should be reso-
lutely cast overboard from the Steamship of Modernity, the image of the
venerable classics that most readily springs to mind is a long row of
plaster busts.

In the same year, 1912, Mayakovsky declared in his article 'Two
Chekhovs' that the young art was fighting against 'this canonisation of
liberal writers whose heavy bronze monuments step on the throat of the
new verbal art as it struggles to liberate itself'. The statue motif that
occurs throughout the poet's works is intimately connected with his
basic themes of struggle between stasis and change, the division of time
into the negative entity 'past/present', on the one hand, and the positive
but forever unattainable 'future', on the other. The huge, heavy, immobile statue as an obstacle to the new life is a central and extremely
personal symbol in Mayakovsky.[3] At the same time, criticism of the 'cult
of the statue' and use of the statue as a metaphor for art that has lost its
vital function and lapsed into a 'fetish' became a commonplace among
the spokesmen of the Russian avant-garde in the years immediately
following the Revolution.

Statues and the early Soviet government

The Soviet of People's Commissars, the new revolutionary government,
did not undertake any spectacular dismantlings of tsarist monuments
comparable to the destruction of the Vendôme Column in Paris in 1871,
although there were certainly suitable candidates at hand, such as the
Alexander Obelisk on Senate Square in front of the Winter Palace, which
was patterned directly on Napoleon's monument to himself. The obvious
political symbolism of these statues, of course, could not escape official
notice. Lenin himself devoted considerable attention to the matter. Published documents indicate that statues were the only cultural issue in the
narrow sense that actually interested the Party leader; as we have already

seen, the conflict over Proletkult was more a matter of principle than a general political issue.

The governmental decree 'On the Monuments of the Republic' of 12 April 1918 declared:

> Monuments erected in honour of tsars and their servants, which have neither historical nor artistic value, shall be removed from squares and streets; some of them to be placed in storehouses and others developed for utilitarian purposes.

Removal of the historically and artistically uninteresting monuments – the qualification is worth noting – was only one side of the matter. The government decided at the same time that the newly appointed committee on statues would

> mobilise artistic forces and organise a broad competition of projects for monuments to commemorate the great days of the Russian socialist revolution.

Thus new symbols were to be erected immediately to replace those of the old regime. The government requested that 'already on May Day some of the uglier idols be dismounted and that the first models of new monuments be put up for the masses to pass their judgement on them'.[4] Numerous documents of 1918 and 1919 indicate that Lenin personally attached great importance to the question. He was deeply irritated that Lunacharsky and the Narkompros statue committee were producing so few new monuments, and he reportedly threatened to have the chairman of the committee arrested, shouting, 'Shame on the saboteurs and dullards!' The obstacles were partly material in nature – the scarcity of metals such as bronze in the middle of the Civil War necessitated the use of provisional materials such as plaster and papier-mâché – and the artistic quality of the projects proposed was also generally considered to be very uneven. However, the relatively meagre and slow production of statues of revolutionary heroes from Radishchev to Blanqui and Bakunin was probably also due to the fact that opinions differed greatly within Narkompros on the intrinsic value of Lenin's initiative. The avantgardists there had no sympathy whatever for projects to erect pseudoclassical portraits of revolutionary heroes on the pedestals recently occupied by 'the idols of the tsars and their servants'.[5]

The avant-garde and iconoclasm

In 'The Manifesto of the Flying Federation of Futurists' (March 1918), the first post-revolutionary document issued by the reorganised futurists, the statue was once again used as a symbol of the art of bourgeois society. According to the signatories David Burlyuk, Vasily Kamensky and Vladimir Mayakovsky, the February Revolution had abolished political slavery and the October Revolution had done away with economic bondage, but the third revolution, a 'Revolution of the Spirit' that would put an end to cultural slavery, had yet to be made. For six months after the establishment of Soviet power the theatres were still showing bourgeois plays, and 'just as before, monuments to generals, princes, mistresses of tsars and lovers of tsarinas place a heavy, dirty foot on the throat of the young streets'.[6]

The image of the oppressive, suffocating bulk of the statue is almost the same as in Mayakovsky's 1912 article cited above. In the winter of 1918–19 *Art of the Commune* published a number of poems and statements made at public gatherings in which Mayakovsky repeatedly used the statue to symbolise the bourgeois 'fetishised' art that continued to exist in what was supposedly a revolutionary society. Perhaps the best known poem from this period is 'Too Early to Celebrate', which includes the following lines:

> If you find a White Guardist,
> You put him against the wall.
> But have you forgotten Raphael?
> Have you forgotten Rastrelli?
> It is time
> to let the bullets
> clatter against the walls of the museums.
> Let throats open fire on the old with their hundred-inch cannons![7]

These and similar utterances aroused violent protests among more conservative artists and museum curators – not very surprising in view of the fact that *Art of the Commune* bluntly and energetically declared its support of 'a dictatorship of the minority in art'. Lunacharsky personally intervened and chastised Mayakovsky for his 'destructive attitudes toward the past'. The poet, however, was not an iconoclast who was in reality about to smash statues or burn down museums. Mayakovsky's 'iconoclasm' is a metaphor for the assault by the cultural revolution on the institutionalised functioning of art.[8]

The chief spokesman for 'the dictatorship of the minority' in art, Nikolay Punin, had more specific opinions about monumental art in official Soviet cultural policy. In the very first issue of *Art of the Commune* he criticised the celebration of the first anniversary of the revolution for being practically indistinguishable from bourgeois or even tsarist mass festivals and for using the same draperies, garlands and lanterns. The fault, however, was not that the working class lacked the imagination to arrange its own celebrations, but that the organisers had imitated old, exhausted ideas and 'prettified' the bourgeois inner city instead of radically altering the urban hierarchy. Like Mayakovsky, Punin was concerned with 'destroying' functions rather than things. At the same time he was writing his articles for *Art of the Commune* this erudite art critic was also working in the Commissariat of Enlightenment to rescue invaluable icon collections from the ravages of civil war. But when the government and Lenin personally pushed through the erection of new statues to replace the old without in the least altering their function, Punin counter-attacked. In connection with the anniversary of the founding of the Paris Commune he published an article entitled 'A Day to Remember' that took up the entire front page of *Art of the Commune*. The memorable day was not the birthday of the Commune, however, but 16 May, the day Gustave Courbet was commissioned by the short-lived revolutionary government to take down the Vendôme Column. Courbet, Punin said, had acted as an exemplary revolutionary artist. True, as a painter he was a realist, but then it was a realism that at one time had represented a break with 'feudal and bourgeois classicism'. What the vice-chairman of IZO wanted to focus attention on instead was the fact of a culturally revolutionary attack on Napoleon's monument of victory:

> To him [Courbet] this monument incarnated not only the monster of militarism but also a certain part of French culture, and when with his typical ingenuity he made ready its bed of straw he was surely doing so in spirit for all of the old art as well, for as a revolutionary and communard he wanted the new, believed in the new. . . .
>
> The great master did not hesitate to raise his hand against the hated and already dead past in the name of the new and living idea.[9]

Courbet is described here almost as a futuristic cultural revolutionary whose assault on 'the already dead past' had lost none of its relevance to the present day. Punin maintained that the Commune's symbolic action on 16 May 1871 was a model for the proletariat and radical artists in

1919 as well – proof that the working class had come to power not to preserve the 'wretched remains' of the past but 'to create something of its own to replace that which in effect had ceased to exist'.

In another article in the avant-garde paper Punin took direct issue with the government's initiative to replace tsarist statues with new ones. As an IZO official who was well aware of the energy Lenin had expended on the project, Punin maintained that immortalising individual heroes was wrong in principle: revolutions were made by the masses, not by great individuals. Pseudo-classical statues of revolutionaries merely served to underscore this fact by transforming 'revered personages' into immobile figures of the same type as the recently removed tsarist monuments. The best and most creative artists, Punin went on, turned their backs on the traditional statue. As an example he mentioned Vladimir Tatlin, who at this time, in the spring of 1919, was working on a completely new and different sort of monument. Here Punin summarised the first drafts of what was to become Tatlin's famous 'tower' project, the *Monument to the Third International*. The principles upon which Tatlin based his project resembled those set forth in Boccioni's manifesto: instead of a stationary figurative statue, Tatlin proposed utilising the simplest geometrical figures in a dynamic, kinetic interaction. The monument was not to be abstractly decorative, however, but a gigantic public building with assembly rooms, a propaganda centre, and so on. The space of the classical sculpture was to be broken up once and for all and the monument was to be integrated into non-aesthetic reality, thus becoming what Boccioni called a 'sculpture of the environment'.[10]

Tatlin's anti-monument

By the autumn of 1920 the first model of Tatlin's 'tower' was ready. It was shown first in Petrograd on the anniversary of the Revolution and then in Moscow in connection with the Eighth Congress of Soviets in December. The model, in the form of two spirals enclosing a cube, a cylinder, a cone and a rotating hemisphere of what was to be a 400-metre-high structure of glass and steel, has in recent years been reconstructed.[11]

In a brochure from the exhibitions in 1920 Punin pointed out three properties of the tower that justify calling it a gigantic *anti*-monument, an avant-garde antithesis to earlier notions of what a monument ought to be. In contrast to the *individual, static* and in the practical sense *useless* pseudo-classical statue, Tatlin's tower was based on the 'material

Vladimir Tatlin
The Work Ahead of Us

The visual arts – our trade – have lacked common basic principles, and the connection between painting, sculpture and architecture has been lost. This has led to individualism, i.e. expressions of merely personal habit and taste, and those artists who have begun working with materials have themselves degraded it to a deviation from the genres of the visual arts; artists have therefore at best decorated the walls in private homes (individual nests) and left behind numerous 'Yaroslavl [railway] Stations' and a mass of now ridiculous forms.

What happened on the social plane in 1917 we accomplished in our art in 1914, when we made 'material, volume and construction' our fundamental notions.

We declare our mistrust toward the eye and subject it to the control of touch.

In 1915 we arranged an exhibition of experimental material models (an exhibition of reliefs and contra-reliefs).

A 1917 exhibition contained numerous examples of combinations of materials based on more complicated studies in which the material as such was bared to reveal movement, tension, and the interrelationship between the two.

In 1918, this study of material, volume and construction enabled us in artistic form to begin combining materials such as iron and glass, the materials of modern classicism, equal in severity to the marble of earlier ages.

In this way it becomes possible to unite purely artistic forms with utilitarian purposes. For example, the project of a Monument to the III International (displayed at the Eighth Congress).

The results of this are models that stimulate invention in creating a new world and force the producers to take control over the forms of everyday life.

Signed by *V. E. Tatlin, T. Shapiro, I. Meyerson, P. Vinogradov*
Moscow, 31 December 1920

From *Daily Bulletin*, No. 13 of the Eighth Congress of Soviets (1921) culture' of non-figurative art and was *collective*, *dynamic* and *utilitarian*: the mobile 'monument' to the Third International was to house the World Parliament and Government offices beneath a news bureau capped by a radio mast. 'Working as a labourer on the three units of the modern plastic consciousness – material, construction and volume', Tatlin's tower provided a magnificent prototype for the production art to be developed at InKhuK.[12]

In one of his rare public statements (on the exhibition at the Congress of Soviets) Tatlin summarised his ideas on the tower. The value of the project, he said in terms that foreshadow the theory of production art, was that it demonstrated the possibility of uniting 'purely artistic forms with utilitarian goals'.[13]

Describing the study of 'material, construction and volume' as the long-term significance of the project, Tatlin compared iron and glass, 'the materials of contemporary classicism', to the marble of antiquity. Such talk of a 'modern classicism' may seem surprising coming from the first real representative of utilitarian art. The connections and parallels between the nascent Soviet Russian art and architecture and the revolutionary neo-classicism of France after 1789 are not coincidental, however, for utopianism, the projection of an idealised picture of antiquity, and the dream of uniting art and science were all central topics in the revolutionary discourses of both 1789 and 1917.[14] It is against this background that Tatlin's remark on iron and glass as the material of a new classicism should be viewed. It is also significant that he chose a monument rather than, say, an apartment house for his utilitarian experiments with materials. If we call the *Monument to the Third International* an 'anti-monument', we must place equal stress on both parts of the compound.

Permanent iconoclasm

Mayakovsky saw Tatlin's tower in 1920, greeting it enthusiastically as 'the first monument without a beard'. There is reason to believe, however, that his defence of the project was the tactical move of a colleague on the beleaguered left front. As we have already seen, in Mayakovsky's aesthetic system the monument was intrinsically negative. In his passionate and ironical 'provisional monument', the poem 'To the Workers of Kursk' (1923) the poet declared that 30,000 miners ('thank God!') cannot each have a statue, nor can the mine itself be immortalised. Pseudo-classical sculptors are not needed here, but neither are Tatlin and his tower next to the real towers of the smokestacks![15] To Mayakovsky, any monument was an attempt to stop time, to hold back the struggle for the future. The poet declared he was even prepared to sacrifice himself in this holy struggle if he stood in the way of the new. As he wrote in 'To the Other Side', a kind of reply to Lunacharsky's criticism of 'Too Early to Celebrate':

> March!
> Under your feet –
> tramp with them! –
> we
> will cast ourselves
> and our creations.
> We summon death in the name of life.

The poet's sacrificial death as a last-ditch effort to rescue the world from the stagnation of the everyday is a central topos in all of Mayakovsky's works.[16] Variants of it are also found in other futurists, however, as in Sergey Tretyakov's poem 'To the Living', which exacts of future generations a promise to blow up the futurists' statues if they get in the way of the new art – and life – of tomorrow.[17] Written in 1923, this poem was one of Tretyakov's last. Like many others, he was moving into a new field that promised great possibilities for the cultural-revolutionary project of transforming life through art: the theatre.

Part II

Theatre as Action

Chapter 4

Theatre as Example

We saw in the preceding section that the Russian avant-garde launched a theoretical and actual attack on the monument as the prototype of bourgeois art. The static, individual and fetishised statue can be said to represent the negative pole in 'left' aesthetics.

Let us now turn to an analysis of what can be regarded as the positive pole of that system: the theatre. In no other art form is the confrontation between art and reality more apparent. And in the dynamic, collective, and utilitarian experimental theatre of the early 1920s the avant-garde seemed closer than ever to realising its utopia of bursting the boundaries of the closed, autonomous work of art and doing away with the opposition between 'life' and 'art'.

Together with Mayakovsky, the Soviet Russian avant-garde writer who gave most attention to the theatre was Sergey Tretyakov. The discussion below frequently takes Tretyakov's work as a point of reference, not because he was a writer of Mayakovsky's genius (much of his writing is of only 'archaeological' interest today), but because he himself was a peculiar melting-pot for a number of typical features of the politicised avant-garde of the 1920s. It is no coincidence that the name Sergey Tretyakov is usually referred to now amid a constellation of others. But these 'others' happened to be some of the most interesting personalities of the age: Mayakovsky, Meyerhold, Eisenstein, Bertolt Brecht. The impatient talent of Tretyakov always seemed to be involved wherever an experiment was under way – in the theatre, in film, in journalism. Between 1922 and 1926 he wrote four plays of his own and reworked three others. All were done on commission from Meyerhold's theatre and the Moscow Proletkult's First Workers' Theatre headed by Sergey Eisenstein. As a critic Tretyakov was an exponent of left avant-garde aesthetics who expressed the ideas of the day with the extremism of the true believer.[1]

The experiments of the Soviet avant-garde laid bare certain basic theatrical problems and made them accessible to critical reflection. The rich theoretical language developed in the manifestos, programmatic pronouncements and criticism of the time, however, was more the ideological superstructure of a particular practice than a separate metalanguage that can be used to describe different types of theatre. But the *questions* the avant-garde posed about how theatre as an art form functions and about the relationship between the stage and the auditorium were so radical that today, seventy years later, they force us to re-examine both the assumptions upon which the theatre is based and the language and methods used to describe it.[2]

Chapter 5

The Semiotics of Theatre

Theatrical doctrines and theatrical theory

The theatre is a complex art form. A theatrical performance includes a number of factors which the director combines to convey his overall vision or message to the spectator. One important function of a general theatrical theory or semiotics is to distinguish the various components of the scenic action or performance. Tadeusz Kowzan has defined thirteen such components, regarding each of them as a separate sign system. These are word, tone, mime, gesture, movement, make-up, hair-style, costume, accessory, decor, lighting, music, and sound effects.[1] Such a list, however, immediately raises the question of how the various components operate as subsystems in the total sign system of the performance. In other words, what happens when these different factors are made to interact on a stage before an audience?

The notion that the theatre is a composite art form does not automatically lead to a single view of the essence of the theatre. On the contrary, the various doctrines of modern theatre could be arranged on a scale with the notion of theatre as a combination of all possible factors at one pole, and the conception that some one factor is its *sine qua non* at the other. An example of the first extreme is of course Wagner's *Gesamtkunstwerk*, the theatre as a synthesis of a number of other art forms. At the other end of the scale we find various purist ambitions to elevate the actor's speech or movements or the script or some other element to the one indispensable kernel of the theatre, that without which what the spectator sees ceases to be theatre. Different purists have consequently felt obliged to proclaim the 'death' of the theatre, although the art itself has continued to develop as before.

The foundations of an undoctrinaire, general theory of the theatre were first sketched out by the Prague structuralists in the 1930s. Pyotr Bogatyr's study of the Czech and Slovak folk theatre derives its significance not only from the unique body of materials upon which it is based, but above all from its consistent application of a semiotic view of the theatre as a form of communication. Articles by other scholars such as Jan Mukařovský and Jindřich Honzl developed the structuralist method in immediate relation to the practice of the Czech avant-garde theatre of the time.[2]

In a 1941 lecture in Prague, Mukařovský formulated certain basic and still valid principles for a structural study of the theatre.[3] He begins with two fundamental elements in Richard Wagner's theory, which can be regarded as the starting point for the past 120 years of Western theatrical aesthetics. These elements are first, the relationship between stage and auditorium, and second, the various components of the action on stage. Both aspects are highly relevant to the description and analysis of Russian theatrical modernism, and I shall therefore briefly summarise Mukařovský's arguments.

First, the components of the action. Mukařovský objects both to the Wagnerian *Gesamtkunstwerk* doctrine and to the different variants of its opposite, purism. While it is true that the theatre is made up of a number of factors or elements that derive from other art forms, such as music, painting, literature, and so on, in the theatre these participate in a whole in which they become intertwined, losing their intrinsic character. To the question whether any specific element of the theatre can be considered absolutely fundamental Mukařovský replies:

> The answer is 'no' if we regard the theatre not only from the standpoint of a certain artistic movement but as a constantly developing and changing phenomenon. Individual developmental stages of the theatre and of particular theatrical movements have, of course, their prevailing components. The dominant component of the theatre is at one time the dramatic text, at another time the actor, at another time the director or even the stage set. . . . And this changeability is made possible only because, as we have said, none of the components is absolutely necessary and fundamental for the theatre.

Thus no individual element of a performance can be isolated as the kernel of the theatre, that piece containing the theatrical 'essence' without which the theatre also disappears. Instead there is a whole in which the significant functions can be shifted, scattered or concentrated to those possible theatrical elements that are being realised at a given moment.

Mukařovský's functional reasoning leads to certain important conclusions. It is sometimes said that, although a theatrical event can have any appearance, the fact that it is happening *on a stage* is the crucial consideration. Here again the theatre is being connected with a material element that in some more or less mystical fashion is the bearer of its essence ('the boards representing the world'). The untenability of this purist dogma becomes evident in the Russian revolutionary theatre, in which performances were given on the streets and in the squares, in factories and on the beds of trucks as well as in ordinary theatre buildings. The theatre cannot be linked to the presence of a stage any more than to any given scenic element. Just as the meaning of a scenic element exists only in relation to other elements, the stage means something only in relation to an auditorium.

The relationship between the stage and the auditorium has nothing to do with a material construction, but is purely functional and can be realised in many different ways. Actors crossing the footlights and playing among the audience have at various times in theatrical history demonstrated this fact. That the stage – auditorium relationship really is only functional and not material is obvious from the following. The pair 'stage – auditorium' can even be realised as the relationship 'actor – spectator' in one and the same person. When children act out theatre for themselves or when an actor rehearses without an audience they have not only an imagined audience but above all themselves as spectators.

To summarise: it can be said that neither the actor nor the text nor the scenery nor the stage nor the auditorium as material facts are necessary to allow us to speak of a theatrical event. What is needed is the *relationship* between the dynamic whole of the scenic elements and the spectator viewing it; in other words, it is the *function of the spectator* that is indispensable. This applies, however, to all types of spectacle – circus or athletic contest as well as theatre. Thus we must make yet another definition before we can claim to have pinpointed the essence of a theatrical event.

The sign function of the theatre

Events that involve the functional pair 'stage' and 'auditorium', that is, the presence of a spectator, are thus not necessarily *theatrical* events. To be theatrical, an event must also point to something beyond itself, represent something, in a way that a boxing match or lecture on anatomy does not do.

Olle Hildebrand has made a useful distinction between the theatre and the two related phenomena of cult rituals and sporting events. The cult differs from the theatre in that there is no separation of spectators and actors, whereas in an athletic contest the difference lies in the fact that what the spectators see is not dominated by the sign function.[4]

It is generally recognised that ritual gave rise to the theatre of antiquity. The development of the theatre as an art form can be regarded as the development of the spectator ingredient and thus the victory of *the theatrical function* over others such as the magical or religious. As Bertolt Brecht puts it: 'Theatre may be said to be derived from ritual, but that is only to say that it becomes theatre once the two have separated . . .'[5] The *sign function* is necessary to distinguish the theatre from, say, the athletic contest, just as the *spectator function* is what distinguishes it from the ritual act. These two functions together constitute the theatrical function, which comes into play when an event is viewed as an artistic sign.

The theatrical function is an example of the aesthetic function analysed in detail by structuralist studies in literature and the arts. With respect to literature, the aesthetic function is usually referred to as 'poetic'. It implies that the words of language are transformed from designations for things and notions in our everyday surroundings into expressions of a (poetic) content that is far broader and much more fluid than everyday language allows. All art forms have a counterpart to this now familiar view of the poetic function of language as a 'secondary' or 'connotative' language that employs the elements of everyday language in a transferred function, in inverted commas, so to speak. The Russian Romantic Lermontov's lyric 'The Sail' does not refer to any real sailing trip, even though it is structured on words designating just such a voyage, nor does Ilya Repin's painting of Lev Tolstoy at the plough document Tolstoy's agricultural experiments at Yasnaya Polyana, even though it is made up of pictorial elements that represent just that.

Especially obvious is the distinction the theatre makes between the practical function of actions and that which they designate or symbolise on the 'secondary' level or special context offered by the theatrical performance. According to an anecdote often used to illustrate this difference between 'life' and 'art', a gentleman in Chicago in 1909 was so upset at seeing Othello strangle Desdemona that he drew his pistol and shot the leading actor. This unfortunate gentleman was unable to understand the aesthetic function in the actor's actions; that is, he was unable to view them as signs of actions rather than as real actions. The consequences of his error were more serious, but the gentleman was in effect making the same mistake as the person who asks what kind of boat Lermontov was writing about or wonders whether the oxen at Yasnaya Polyana were not in fact larger.

The aesthetic function comes into play when we view something as art. *And to view something as art is to view it as a sign for something*. We can watch someone being mistreated on the stage and still react positively, because we regard the actions on stage not as real actions, but as meaningful signs for something else. If we thought an assault really were taking place we would interfere, and if we did not discover until later that we had witnessed real violence, we would be revolted.

The theatre is one form of communication in which the nature of art as sign becomes particularly apparent. The semiotician Yury Lotman says that 'the world, when it becomes a theatrical world, reorganises itself according to the laws of theatrical space, entering which, things become the signs of things'.[6] Perhaps it should only be added that things do not entirely cease being things when they become signs. It was precisely *the tension* that arises between the various functions that became an important object of experimentation in the Soviet Russian avant-garde theatre.

Thus everything is transformed when it comes on stage, when it is put in an artistic, theatrical context. There is no material transformation here, of course, but a change in *function*. Objects, people, movements, words – everything becomes theatre when someone views it *as theatre* rather than as a lecture platform, a furniture warehouse, or a room in which to live. This transformation, which consists of the appearance of the theatrical function as the dominant, ultimately depends on the spectators. If they do not make a functional change in their viewing, there is no artistic communication, and they cannot understand the message the stage is sending, let alone evaluate it. This is what happened to the gentleman who shot an actor in the belief he was aiming at Othello.

Stage, auditorium, society

Thus the spectator, or rather the fact of the spectator's presence, is a prerequisite for the realisation of the theatrical function. In this sense the spectator is a co-creator of each theatrical performance. The same is actually true of the reader of a poem or the viewer of a painting, but owing to the special form of the theatre, the tense relationship between work of art and receiver becomes especially palpable in the confrontation between stage and auditorium.

Mukařovský's analysis of the components of the scenic work of art led to the conclusion that the 'essence' of the theatre must be sought in the theatrical function. The starting point for this argument was a critique of Wagner's doctrine of the *Gesamtkunstwerk*. Richard Wagner may also be taken as the source for the second set of problems treated by Mukařovský in his 1941 lecture which are of crucial interest to a study of the Russian avant-garde: the relationship between the theatrical work of art, its audience, and society outside the theatre.

A theatrical performance is a message to the spectator. But who is the spectator? Who is sitting in the auditorium? Here Mukařovský puts his finger on a central yet seldom explicitly expressed basic concept in the modern theatre that might be called *the myth of the representative auditorium*. By that I mean the notion that the superior social significance of the theatre as compared to other art forms is thought to derive from the fact that the audience in the auditorium represents the collective *as a whole*. This myth has given rise to many grandiose dreams of a theatre capable of speaking to all of society and recreating the ideological and moral unity that the theatre of antiquity or the Middle Ages was thought to embody.

> But it is not the entire society of this or that time, this or that people, which frequents the theatre, especially the contemporary theatre; rather it is an audience, that is, a community, often socially heterogeneous (let us not consider social strata alone but also status, age, etc.) but tied together by a bond of receptivity for the art of the theatre.[7]

'Receptivity for the art of the theatre' sometimes combines with or is even eclipsed by other interests related to politics, etiquette, and so forth, but belonging to the audience would still seem to presuppose receptivity to the language of the theatre. It is only this audience that in turn becomes the mediator between the work of art, the performance, and society. The theatrical audience, however, cannot be regarded as a homogeneous unit either. As Mukařovský points out, each theatre with an artistic profile of its own also has an audience of its own which knows the artistic stamp of this theatre and views each new performance in relation to preceding ones.

The connection between the auditorium and society, then, is far more indirect than many in the theatre have imagined. The idea that the spectators in the auditorium somehow directly represent the entire collective (society, people) is of Romantic origin. In their art, Romantic artists aspired – as a compensation or as a social utopia – to present the liberty, equality and fraternity that the victorious bourgeoisie advocated in theory but denied in practice to the other classes. Even before the Romantics, Jean-Jacques Rousseau had held up the theatre of antiquity as the prototype of an art that set aside class barriers and created a true democratic collectivity.[8]

In his 1849 manifesto *Art and Revolution*, Richard Wagner advanced – with no reference to Rousseau – the grandiose notion of the theatre as a meeting place for *the entire people*. This may be said to mark the birth of the idea of modern people's theatre. To Wagner the revolutionary, the history of the theatre since Greek antiquity was one long story of decay and prostitution. Never after the Attic democracy had the theatre fulfilled the same social function or been so wholly the concern of the entire people (Wagner forgot for the moment that Athenian society was built on slave labour and that women were not admitted into the theatre):

> This people, streaming in its thousands from the State-assembly, from the Agora, from land, from sea, from camps, from distant parts, – filled with its thirty thousand heads the amphitheatre. To see the most pregnant of all tragedies, the 'Prometheus', came they; in this Titanic masterpiece to see the image of themselves, to read the riddle of their own actions, to fuse their own being and their own communion with that of their god. . . .

In Wagner's view, the Greek tragedy was a unique manifestation and confirmation of the community of the entire collective:

> For in tragedy he [the citizen of Athens] found himself again, – nay, found the noblest part of his own nature united with the noblest characteristics of the whole nation; and from his inmost soul, as it there unfolded itself to him, proclaimed the Pythian oracle. At once both God and Priest, glorious godlike man, one with the Universal, the Universal summed up in him. . . .[9]

Thus the classical Greek theatre as an expression of the original Athenian democracy was Wagner's ideal. The goal of the 1848–9 revolution in Germany, however, was not a restoration of the past. Only a real social revolution introducing a new historical epoch could return art and the theatre to their former place at the centre of society.

What, exactly, was the relationship between art and revolution in

Wagner's utopia? What he was talking about was not an art that mirrored social reality, much less art that agitated politically. The revolution would liberate art and restore to it its social necessity. When the German revolution failed to materialise, art instead was *ascribed* social necessity on the model of the Greek ideal. In reality art became a substitute for a true transformation of society, a compensatory sphere. The 'democratic' amphitheatre of the Bayreuth opera, which lacked the boxes and rows of the court theatres, was to afford the spectators the possibility of fusing with the world of the work of art and, at least for a few hours, an opportunity to experience the community and liberty denied them by the class society outside.

For the time being, we need not concern ourselves with Wagner's impact on Russian theatrical aesthetics.[10] The important point is that throughout Europe, not least in Russia beginning with Stanislavsky, all reformers of the theatre shared the faith in the power of theatre that flowed from the Wagnerian notion of the audience as representative of all society. The idea of the people's theatre, especially as developed in Germany and France in the late nineteenth century – the dream of creating a great, dramatic, and 'unifying' theatre for mass audiences – is inconceivable without Wagner's programme. In 1901, the young Max Reinhardt envisaged as a future goal

> ... a very large theatre for a great art of monumental effects, a festival theatre, detached from everyday life, a house of light and solemnity, in the spirit of the Greeks, not merely for Greeks, but for the great art of all epochs, in the shape of an amphitheatre, without curtain or sets, and in the centre, totally relying on the pure effect of personality, totally focused on the word, the actor, in the middle of the audience, and the audience itself, transformed into *the people*, drawn into, become a part of, the action of the play.[11]

Even more Wagnerian were the critic Julius Bab's remarks on the occasion of the fifth anniversary of the Berlin Volksbühne in 1919:

> The theatre has everywhere arisen as the manifestation of a common emotion, a need of inspiration experienced together by an entire collective, an entire people ... the stage loses its life, its meaning and its *raison d'être* if it abandons its origins and ceases to be *an expression, intensified through the forms of festival, of the common experience of a community, a people.* .... Aid is to be had from only one quarter: the theatre house must be rebuilt from the ground up, the

audience must be organised, *the bond between people and theatre must be restored.*[12]

The contradictions in the Wagnerian notion of the folk theatre that Bab glosses over out of enthusiasm for the new theatre building in Berlin, however, remained unresolved. They recur in the theatre of revolutionary agitation in Soviet Russia after 1917, in Erwin Piscator's political theatre, and in rituals of class conciliation such as Gémier's 'republican festivals' in the 1910s and 1920s or the Nazi German monumental plays, the so-called *Thingspiele.*

Gémier's mass festivals harked back not only to the Greek tragedy that Wagner took as his model, but even more to Rousseau's programme for the republican festival. The unity of stage and auditorium (the auditorium in turn being regarded as directly representing the people, nation, collective) is manifested in the mass festival not only in the common experience of art (as in Wagner), but through the active participation of the whole audience in the play:

> In brief, it is not only the stage that tells a story of unity; the whole ceremony is living proof of this unity: actor and spectator become one.[13]

In his book *Théâtre du peuple* (1903) Romain Rolland argued both for the artistic people's theatre in what might be called a 'Wagnerian spirit', and, referring directly to Rousseau and to the fêtes during the French Revolution, for the huge mass festivals. The book was translated into Russian in 1910 and came out in a new edition in 1919 in connection with the great wave of revolutionary mass spectacles that swept over Russia during the Civil War.[14]

I will touch upon the theory and practice of the revolutionary mass theatre at several points below. Our real subject, however, is *the professional avant-garde theatre* – Constructivism, or to use a slightly more vague concept, 'left theatre' and its development in the 1920s. As specific examples I have selected the Moscow productions of Sergey Tretyakov's plays of 1922–6.

One interesting feature of Tretyakov's plays and their productions is their intense preoccupation with the *relationship between stage and auditorium.* Theoretical writings by Meyerhold and Eisenstein and Tretyakov himself planned, described and evaluated these experiments. At the same time and in part as a result of the experiments, the radical Soviet Russian theatre began to theorise on the nature of the audience and became increasingly aware of the many intermediate links that exist between stage, auditorium and society. As a result, the myth of the representative auditorium disintegrated. Below we shall trace the development that ended in the crisis of the political agitational theatre.

Even if it is a myth or illusion that the audience in the auditorium directly represents the collective as a whole and that the theatre speaks through it to all of 'society', 'the nation', or 'the working class', this of course does not mean that the myth itself is not a reality. On the contrary, it has figured prominently in the history of the nineteenth- and twentieth-century theatre precisely as *a myth*, an ideological fact. To provide a background to our analysis of the Soviet Russian avant-garde theatre, therefore, it may be appropriate first to compare the main concepts of theatre aesthetics in the preceding period on the basis of their explicit or implicit view of the audience.

Chapter 6

Stage and Auditorium in the Russian Modernist Theatre

Although most currents in Russian theatre from naturalism in the 1890s to constructivism in the 1920s seem to have embraced the myth of the representative auditorium, this in no way means that they had a common notion as to *how* the stage would confront this auditorium. On the contrary, the 'representative' view of the audience served as the starting point for a number of widely different conceptions of the ideal relationship between stage and auditorium.

Theatrical modernism in Russia developed as a reaction against the naturalism of Stanislavsky and the first period of the Moscow Art Theatre (MAT). It is therefore against this background that the various systems that were introduced during the first decades of the century should be discerned and approached. I will schematically contrast Stanislavsky's naturalism with two other pre-revolutionary theatrical conceptions – Meyerhold's early 'stylisation' and the 'ritual' people's theatre – and then go on to consider revolutionary avant-gardism as represented by Meyerhold's and Eisenstein's constructivism.[1]

Three types of theatre

The approach taken by the various theatrical conceptions toward the ideal relationship between the stage and the auditorium can be described on the basis of the following distinctive features or variables:

(1) *marking/abolishing* the footlights;
(2) *congruence/incongruence* between the worlds of the stage and the auditorium;
(3) the direction of the theatre *into/out of* the world of the stage.

The footlights were taboo in naturalistic theatre. The actors in Stanislavsky's famous productions of Chekhov et al. were to play as if they were in a room from which the fourth wall had been removed; the spectators were to be led to believe they were viewing 'a slice of life'. But this did not mean that the footlights had been abolished. They were in fact strongly *marked*, although negatively. The fourth wall was transformed into an invisible glass wall that was as impenetrable as the boundary between reality and its mirror image.

The life of the stage was also the life of the auditorium and the actors. The congruence between stage and auditorium was observable even on the level of setting, but more important was the *congruence* or identity that was created by psychological realism and cut across ethnic or historical differences.

For all this realism of setting and ethnographic verisimilitude, Stanislavsky's theatre was none the less oriented *inward*, toward the world of the stage. Through identification with the characters the audience projected their feelings and conflicts on to the stage. And it was there, in that fictive world, that such conflicts were resolved. For Stanislavsky, the cathartic experience in art was the end for which even the most meticulous reproduction was only a means.

Stanislavsky regarded the word 'theatrical' as a term of abuse. To him it meant artifice, overacting, the incapacity for realistic characterisation on the stage. In a series of meticulously well-rehearsed productions around the turn of the century (Chekhov, Ibsen, Gorky), his Moscow Art Theatre overcame the 'automatism' of a theatrical language that had stagnated in declamation and the unconscious repetition of histrionic clichés. But once realism had at least potentially been established in the Russian theatre, 'theatricality' could regain semantic vitality on a new level as an *alternative* to realism in its naturalistic form.

Thus mature realism on the stage bore within it the seeds of revolt. In his 1902 article 'The Unnecessary Truth', symbolist poet and critic Valery Bryusov attacked MAT's aesthetics and defended 'conventional' (*uslovnaya*) theatricality, that is, the right of art to refuse to imitate reality and instead to speak its own language.[2] 'Conventional' or 'stylised' came in fact to designate the theatre that Vsevolod Meyerhold developed in close conjunction with the symbolist poets after his break with MAT in 1905. Meyerhold often pointed to the deliberate abbreviations and signals in the Chinese theatre, which did not attempt to imitate reality but could describe a long journey with a single step or a note on a flute. In the new 'drama of allusions' of such playwrights as Maeterlinck, Blok and Andreyev that Meyerhold staged after 1905, symbols in the broader sense were central, serving as sensual representations of a metaphysical reality.

What does the 'stylised theatre' look like if we schematise it on the basis of the variables presented above? At first, in a deliberate effort to contrast with the 'peep-show' of naturalism, the stylised theatre employed shallow, relief-like stage designs, and then went on to bring the actors out on to an expanded proscenium, to allow entrances from the auditorium, and so on. In both cases there is a clear *marking* (negative and positive, respectively) of the boundary between stage and auditorium. This was made all the more obvious by the fact that this boundary at times did not coincide with the traditional footlights but was a purely functional, mobile, 'psychological' border (as in the 1914 production of Alexander Blok's *The Fairground Booth*).

As to the second distinctive feature, there was quite clearly *incongruence* between stage and auditorium in Meyerhold's stylised theatre. There was no room on stage for psychology or realism of setting. The reality of art in this system differed radically from that of the everyday and obeyed laws (rhythmicised speech, symbolic colours, plastic movement) that were peculiar to it and quite 'unnatural' from the ordinary point of view.

Finally, there is the third variable, the one I have termed the 'direction' of the theatre either into the world of the stage or away from the stage out into material reality. The stylised theatre was oriented *inward*. Life was viewed as a dream or an illusion, whereas art provided knowledge of a 'higher' reality. Meyerhold's theatre showed the pedestrian everyday in a spectral or grotesque light, while the true, 'higher' reality could be glimpsed peeking out from behind double masks and the wings or existed only as hope and desire.

The 'ritual' people's theatre, the third pre-revolutionary theatrical conception I have chosen to describe according to the typological scheme above, is not rooted as concretely in theatrical history as the other notions. For a long time it remained a utopia, but as such, on the other hand, it played a prominent role.

The programme of the people's theatre as developed by Romain Rolland had two parts: there was first of all the magnificent spectacle that would fuse the collective together through a common aesthetic experience *à la* Wagner, and then there were the mass festivals that were to unite the collective in a great ritual. The question of the relationship between the theatre and ritual was made topical at about this time especially by Nietzsche's *The Birth of Tragedy*, which elaborated upon the view of the Greek theatre advanced by Wagner (to whom, incidentally, the book was dedicated). For Nietzsche as well the ancient Greek tragedy was a theatre for *all* citizens, for all of society, and spectators and actors theoretically belonged to a single whole.

Nietzsche's great idea was to reconstruct the development of tragedy out of ritual and to retrace the original 'Dionysian' element which had later been suppressed by the 'Apollonian' one. In the Dionysian festival there was no distinction at all between spectators and actors, and Nietzsche's description of ritual ecstasy took the form of a utopia that was if anything even more magnificent than Wagner's notion of the tragedy:

> In song and in dance man expresses himself as a member of a higher community; he has forgotten how to walk and speak and is on the way toward flying into the air, dancing. His very gestures express enchantment. Just as the animals now talk, and the earth yields milk and honey, supernatural sounds emanate from him, too: he feels himself a god, he himself now walks about enchanted, in ecstasy, like the gods he saw walking in his dreams. He is no longer an artist, he has become a work of art. . . .[3]

Nietzsche's vision of the Dionysian festival – which not only fuses together all participants but also abolishes *the distinction between audience, artist and work of art* – attracted many enthusiastic interpreters in Russia. The symbolist poet Vyacheslav Ivanov took Nietzsche as the starting point for his defence of the ritual theatre. Ivanov insisted on the necessity of finding the ritual sources from which theatre has arisen. The community of the cult would enable man to transcend the dualistic split between body and soul, matter and spirit, for the distinction the theatre drew between spectators and players and between stage and auditorium was a manifestation of the same split.

The ritual theatre was and remained a totally utopian project, at least until the October Revolution. The ideas Ivanov advanced in a series of articles from 1904 to 1917, however, had a strong impact and generated parallels in the works of other Russian followers of Nietzsche. The most prominent example is the composer Alexander Scriabin, author of the synthetic symphonic work *Prometheus: The Poem of Fire* (1909–10) and the colossal *Mystery*, for which he completed only a first draft.

Although Ivanov's programme was utopian and theoretical, it can also be described on the basis of the distinctive features introduced above. As we have seen earlier, the ritual act that Ivanov regarded as the ideal of the theatre is characterised by a repression of the function of the spectator. 'The footlights' – that is, the division into actors and spectators, stage and auditorium – is *not marked* either positively or negatively. The worlds of the stage and of the auditorium – the ideal and reality – are *incongruent*. Finally, the ritual theatre is directed *inward* toward the sphere of the stage, since the participants in the ritual act were to leave drab reality behind and enter into a new community: to quote the poet, *a realibus ad realiora* ('from the real to the more real').[4]

Let us now compare the three types of theatre outlined above. It should perhaps be emphasised that we are speaking here of relatively abstract models of the ideal relationship between stage and auditorium as exemplified in naturalism, the stylised theatre, and the utopian programme of ritual theatre. We are thus not claiming to provide a description of Stanislavsky's and the early Meyerhold's specific theatrical practice, or of Ivanov's theatrical concepts. In reality, we must allow for various mixed types, fluctuations between different alternatives, and so on. If a schematic grid superimposed on an object *simplifies*, however, it also *clarifies*, and therein lies its heuristic value.

The views discussed here of the ideal relationship between stage and auditorium can be expressed with the help of a few simple graphic symbols. We can designate the two halves of the theatre – the stage and the auditorium – with two simple figures representing the stage to the left and the auditorium to the right. The shapes of the figures are of course arbitrary, since the relations we are dealing with are purely functional and not material.

Distinctive feature 1 – *marking/abolishing* the footlights – is indicated by separating or joining the two halves of the theatre.

Distinctive feature 2 – *congruence/incongruence* between the worlds of stage and auditorium – is shown by figures of identical or different shape.

Distinctive feature 3 – the orientation of the theatre *into/out of* the world of the stage – is indicated by an arrow.

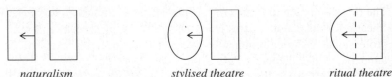

naturalism   *stylised theatre*   *ritual theatre*

Thus in naturalism, for example, the footlights are *marked* (the two halves are separated), there is *congruence* between stage and auditorium (the former 'mirrors' the latter), and the theatre brings the spectator *into* the world of the stage (its goal is to promote identification and catharsis). The stylised theatre differs from naturalism in that the worlds of stage and auditorium are *incongruent*: art does not imitate reality but obeys quite different laws. The ritual theatre strives to abolish the boundary between the worlds of stage and auditorium, and the two halves fuse together. The world of art and the stage – which differs from that of drab, mundane reality – is dominant and draws the spectator *into* the sphere of the stage.

In an earlier version of this typology I chose Nikolay Yevreinov's 'theatre-in-life', rather than ritual theatre, to represent the third type. The change would seem to demand an explanation.[5] Yevreinov was a theoretician and producer who made a passionate study of all forms of theatricalisation and ritualisation in human life. According to him, acting, dissimulating, being something one is not, was an elementary human instinct that was most fully satisfied in the richly orchestrated theatrical event. Satisfaction could be had by watching as a spectator – through empathy with the dissimulation of others or in the totality of a monodrama – but it was even more complete for the participant in a play.

Yevreinov's conception of the 'theatricalisation of life' had certain features in common with the ritual theatre. Its starting point, however, was not ritual but *play*. According to Yevreinov's notion, all spectators could at least theoretically become participants, just as in the ritual theatre. In contrast to the latter, however, Yevreinov was anxious to preserve the presence of the spectator: the element of play in which the theatrical instinct found expression lay in the *tension* between participating and viewing. In our discussion below of Yevreinov's mass spectacle of 1920, *The Storming of the Winter Palace*, we shall see how close he came to the idea of ritual theatre (or, perhaps, to *playing* ritual theatre).

The people's theatre before 1917

The first discussion in Russia of 'people's theatre', by which was meant 'theatre for the people', dates from the 1890s, when amateur and semi-professional theatrical companies were started under the aegis of the temperance and 'People's Palace (*narodny dom*) movements. In 1902 there were 102 such theatrical societies, and they rapidly increased to

361 by 1905 and to about 420 by 1909. The artistic ambitions of these theatres, which were led by liberal educators, were as a rule modest, productions tending to be limited to popular comedies and adapted versions of the lighter works of such playwrights as Ostrovsky and Gogol. The government gave the people's theatre movement economic support in the hope that plays would inhibit not only drinking but also – and more importantly – participation in politics, the unions, and other such 'mischief'. Theatres were at the same time closely supervised and governed by special censorship regulations that allowed Gorky's plays, for example, to be staged for the affluent audience of the Moscow Art Theatre but banned from the People's Palaces.[6]

Although it had its limitations, this popular movement laid the foundation for the broad interest in the theatre that was harnessed by such organisations as Proletkult after the October Revolution. At first it did not feel the influence of the people's theatre ideology formulated by Wagner's Russian admirers. This theory was adopted by the artistic intelligentsia, whose slogan 'theatre for the people' as often as not actually meant 'the people for the theatre'. The breakthrough of the people's theatre ideology in Russia after 1905 had less to do with an expansion of the existing philanthropic and temperance theatres than with the crisis of symbolism and the intelligentsia's self-criticism after the abortive revolution.[7]

The symbolist poet Vyacheslav Ivanov's grandiose dream of a collective, liberating ritual was a religious utopia in which art was allotted the vital social role of reconciling all contradictions. In 1906 Ivanov envisaged a ritual theatre in which the entire people would participate:

> The theatres of the chorus tragedies, the comedies and the mysteries must become the breeding-ground for the creative, or prophetic, self-determination of the people; only then will be resolved the problem of fusing actors and spectators in a single orgiastic body; . . .
>
> And only, we may add, when the choral voice of such communities becomes a genuine referendum of the true will of the people will political freedom become a reality.[8]

Ivanov was by no means the only believer in a new, ritual theatre. Contributors to the anthology *Theatre. A Book on the New Theatre* (1908) included not only the symbolists Bryusov and Sologub, but also Anatoly Lunacharsky. Nietzschean, Bolshevik, Bogdanovist, subsequently a founder of Proletkult and a People's Commissar of Enlightenment, Lunacharsky dreamed of a future society in which socialism would unite with religion and 'the temples wold be transformed into theatres and the theatres into temples'. Ivanov's fellow poet Andrey Bely, however, doubted the feasibility of this beautiful utopian idea of an all-uniting ritual festival. He wrote:

> Just imagine a lady of high society, a stock-exchange shark, a worker and a Privy Councillor dressing up in white gowns and entering the temple to be fused together in ritual ecstasy! . . . I am sure we will not be saying the same prayers.

As long as society is rent by class contradictions and religious controversies, all talk of ritual theatre is absurd. 'The temple', Bely concluded sarcastically, 'will remain the [Imperial] Mariia Theatre, and rhetoric will remain rhetoric.'[9]

Meyerhold, the only contributor to the anthology who was professionally employed in the theatre, was coolest of anyone toward the idea of abolishing the boundary between spectators and actors. He agreed with the symbolists' criticism of the naturalist theatre and shared the view that the theatre should be a place for metaphysical experiences, but in his opinion such experiences arose out of the *encounter* between the creativity of the actor and the imagination of the spectator. In the stylised theatre

> the spectator should not forget for a moment that an actor is *performing* before him, and the actor should never forget that he is performing before an audience. . . .[10]

With the exception of the essays by Bely and Meyerhold, who – as he would always continue to do – defended the professionalism of the theatre, the *Theatre* anthology still became something of a manifesto of the ritual people's theatre. It was soon countered by a group of Marxist critics in another anthology, *The Crisis of Theatre*, whose authors attacked the mystical vision of a ritual theatre abolishing all class barriers and complained that the realistic, socially critical repertory had by now been forgotten even at Stanislavsky's MAT. The realistic and politically progressive theatre which they proposed as a solution to the crisis, however, patently derived itself from Wagner's vision of the great, democratic drama.[11]

Thus the ground was already broken when Romain Rolland's *Théâtre du peuple* with its proposed mass spectacles was published in Russian in 1910. Until the revolutionary year of 1917, however, all plans for future popular festive rituals and mass spectacles remained mere utopias. As far as the theatre was concerned, of course, the most significant effect of the February Revolution was the abolition of the censorship. In the private theatres this led to a wave of 'daring' comedies and Rasputin plays that merely served to accentuate the commercialist spirit of the sector, while the previously strictly censured temperance and People's Palace theatres were now able – when their liberal or Social democratic administrators so wished – to offer a deliberately political repertory. A thoroughly new type of ambulating 'street theatre' and theatricalised forms of gatherings could be observed in the wave of demonstrations and mass meetings generated by the new political freedom of the spring of 1917. Here were the beginnings of the great proletarian mass spectacles of the next few years.

The people's theatre utopia after the October Revolution

One of the first theoretical texts published by the Theatre Section of Narkompros (TEO) was Wagner's *Art and Revolution*. In the foreword, the recently appointed Commissar of Enlightenment proclaimed that, like the Communist Manifesto of 'our brilliant teachers Marx and Engels', this brochure by 'the no less brilliant Richard Wagner' was a product of the German Revolution of 1848. Today it was as topical as ever before, Lunacharsky emphasised, and he recommended that it be studied 'by both artists and the victorious workers' democracy'. The people's theatre and the mass spectacle were soon further popularised by the reprinting of another book, Romain Rolland's *Théâtre du peuple*. It carried a foreword by Vyacheslav Ivanov, who in 1918 was employed by TEO.[12]

The Russian director who was most strongly attracted to the people's theatre programme of Wagner and Rolland was Stanislavsky's beloved student, the leader of MAT's First Studio, Yevgeny Vakhtangov. With support from the Commissariat of Enlightenment, in the 1918–19 season Vakhtangov launched a project for a People's Theatre in Moscow with a repertory of classical plays to be staged in a monumental style. As an alternative to open-air productions in the spirit of Rolland, Vakhtangov even wanted to transform the Bolshoi into a People's Theatre. None of these plans materialised, however, and only a few productions were shown, in a theatre of moderate size with 520 seats.[13]

The first programme with a truly utopian ring to it for a Theatre of the Revolution came from the Proletkult movement and one of its leaders, Platon Kerzhentsev. His book *The Creative Theatre* was first published

Proletkult Theatre: 'The Legend'
Description of a production of the Staro-Gorki Proletkult in 1919.

A stuffy auditorium with a low ceiling. A small stage. Neither footlights nor a prompter. Grey cloth has been hung from the stage into the auditorium, separating a part of it from the spectators and concealing the side exits. Directly opposite us is a grey wall. On stage – semi-darkness. Tensely attentive silence. Growing slowly louder, a buzz of approaching voices of men, women, children. Straight through the auditorium a group of tired, hungry women passes with a quiet moan in the direction of the wall. Children run after them. The men appear. Bent under the burden of poverty, their movements accompanied by a quiet lament, they walk slowly along, steadily straining toward the grey wall. Among them is a group who are also bent but still spirited and strong. The women come crawling on their knees, crying 'Bread, give us bread!'. They carry little babies in their arms. They hold out their hands. They beg for help. The men mutter sternly. The front ranks press against the wall. Silence.

Now one voice begins a prayer: 'Great Lord above, you see the suffering of the people. You see that we haven't the strength to go on.' Other voices join in, and the whole crowd pray on their knees to the mysterious God behind the grey wall.

The prayer falls silent. Its last sounds are joined from behind the wall by the strains of a waltz. It becomes dark. A brightly lit window appears in the wall, through which whirling couples can be seen on the other side. Richly attired men and women flash by the window. Some of the people in the crowd raise their heads. They look. The couples pass in front of the window and see the crowd. Moving among them are lackeys bearing platters of delicacies. The crowd hear an idle bunch of revellers contemptuously criticising their tired faces and ragged, dirty clothing. There is muffled murmur from the crowd. And the bourgeois become frightened, but someone calms them: the workers are stupid and timid. They are unorganised and will never dare attack Capital. They have a strong faith in the divine origin of the wall.

The murmur of the men becomes threatening. They advance slowly. But it has become dark, and again they are confronted by the strong wall separating them from the Unknown.

An agitator tries to talk the crowd into destroying the legend. The men believe him, but the timid women stop those who are ready for struggle. Still, a group of the bolder ones attack the wall.

A luxurious room. The Conference Room of the Supreme Council of the World Bourgeoisie. The ruler is delivering a report to the Council on the disturbances among the workers and on the appearance of agitators in their ranks. The bourgeoisie devises a plan to forestall an uprising: to reinforce the army, arrest the instigators, send in their own agitators, muster forth the arguments of science and especially religion.

The crowd hear all this and, more and more aroused, they throw themselves on the enemy. Again the wall rises up. But after a first retreat from it, the bold ones again charge forward, and everyone follows them. Soldiers appear. They repulse the first ranks, but they can no longer stop the attack. A preacher attempts to restrain them with smooth-tongued speeches about the Kingdom of God. The women waver, but the leaders rush forward and with mighty blows rip down the wall. The wall has fallen. The sun shines brightly. On the hill with a hammer in his hand is a mighty and daring worker. He summons the crowd into the distance, toward the rising Sun. His call resounds powerfully:

> Forward, forward to socialism!
> Our path is difficult, and many are the obstacles,
> But the hour is near when we will find our
> > Fatherland,
> And the word man will be replaced by the word
> > brother.

The strains of the Internationale echo mightily. The Sun is blazing. Red banners flash and glow.

The audience joins in the singing of the hymn.

Quoted in Platon Kerzhentsev, *The Creative Theatre*, 4th edition (Petrograd: Gosizdat, 1920).

---

in 1918 and went through five editions by 1923; it was translated into German as early as 1922.[14]

Combining formal eclecticism and idealistic proletarian ideology, Kerzhentsev's 'creative theatre' project developed directly out of the people's theatre programme from Wagner to Rolland and beyond, especially from that part of it that tended toward the popular ritual in which there were no passive spectators but only active participants. Through the October Revolution, Kerzhentsev maintained, the social prerequisites for the realisation of this programme had been created for the first time in history. Although the theatre in bourgeois societies had been affected during the past few decades by reformers who had turned their backs on commercialism and created great artistic performances, these changes meant little, since they had not attacked 'the disastrous division between stage and auditorium' that isolated the actors and held the spectators passive, depriving them 'of any possibility of developing their theatrical instinct and creativity'.

The German *Volksbühnebewegung*, which staged 'good theatre for the people', was rejected by Kerzhentsev as a philanthropic initiative that was entirely incapable of liberating the theatre from its bourgeois dualism. What was needed was not a series of theatrical reforms but a *theatrical revolution*. Not until October 1917, however, had the utopia become feasible, for the precondition of 'creative theatre' was the abolition of the boundary between manual and intellectual labour, between the artist and his audience. The Proletkult theorists believed that such a change was just around the corner.

Kerzhentsev drew upon a variety of sources for models of the revolutionary mass theatre: from his own experience with mass pageants in England and the United States, from Rolland's descriptions of French and Swiss popular festive dramas, from the commemorative festivals of the French Revolution. Theoretically as well Kerzhentsev's programme was a conglomerate of earlier ideas. There is an obvious influence from the 'ritual' people's theatre utopia. The very name 'creative' was one of Ivanov's catchwords, and of course the theatrical instinct to which Kerzhentsev repeatedly referred was a cornerstone in Yevreinov's aesthetic programme.

Kerzhentsev, however, maintained that the October Revolution had imparted an entirely new content to all the forms of theatre which he admitted gleaning from various epochs and societies. The socialist society would abolish the difference between artist and audience, and the road to this transformation lay through pure *proletarian* cultural work, not through the activisation of some diffuse 'people'. Once 'people' was replaced by 'proletariat', however, Kerzhentsev was prepared to accept the 'ritual' community as well as the great, unifying 'Wagnerian' spectacle, both of which were based on the notion of the auditorium representing the entire collective (now the working class rather than the 'people').

The appeal of the people's theatre utopia as the ideological base for stage reform after the Revolution was very strong. It influenced a wide variety of directors, from the highly professional experimenter Meyerhold – who until the February Revolution in 1917 had been working at the Imperial theatres in Petrograd and conducting research on acting technique in his studio – to young enthusiasts in the Proletkult movement.

The traditionalist and/or established stages – for example, the Maly Theatre and the MAT in Moscow, the (formerly Imperial) Aleksandrinsky and the Bolshoy Dramatic Theatres in Petrograd – gave a wide berth to the 'left-wing' mixture of symbolist utopianism, futurism and political agitation, but were careful to orient their repertories toward classics that were thematically 'in tune with' the revolution. A special case was the Kamerny Theatre in Moscow, led by Alexander Tairov. The Kamerny continued with great success to develop its own form of pure, neo-classical theatricalism based on a strict separation of the 'art' of the stage and the 'reality' of the auditorium. Tairov was also the only voice sharply objecting to the revolutionised symbolist utopia of Kerzhentsev et al. In his polemical book *Notes of a Director* (1920) Tairov stressed the autonomy of the theatre as the precondition of its functioning as a means of aesthetic communication. Anticipating almost verbatim the remarks of Brecht (see above p. 43), with whom he otherwise had little in common, Tairov stated that there was no way – or need – to return theatre to its ritual sources without giving up its essence:

> The actor as priest and the audience as a chorus of believers – such was the embryonic form of *pre*-classical theatre. But as soon as the theatre began to be aware of itself, as soon as it began to take shape, to form itself into an independent art, it gradually reduced the spectator's participation in its activity. . . .

Tairov clearly pointed out the links between Ivanov's ritual act and Kerzhentsev's 'collective creativity': both wished for the same return to the ritual sources, 'only with different ideological content'. In opposition to this, Tairov defended what we have called the theatrical function: the sign function and the presence of the observing spectator as a counterpart to the performing actor. The true future of the art was in the strengthening of the theatrical function, or, in Tairov's own words in the 'Theatricalisation of the Theatre'.[15]

In 1920, however, Tairov's was a rather solitary voice. When in the same year Kerzhentsev published the fourth edition of *The Creative Theatre*, he stated not without justification that 'much of what seemed a utopia two years ago now appears to be on the way to becoming reality'.[16]

At the First All-Russian Congress of Workers' and Peasants' Theatre held in Moscow on 17–26 November 1919, reports from across the country had shown that the theatre and especially the revolutionary mass spectacle had become a central element in the public life of the new Soviet state. The mass spectacle, which was often arranged by amateur groups under the leadership of the local Proletkult, followed the guidelines sketched out by Kerzhentsev. The repertory was dominated by condensed chronicle plays portraying revolutionary history from the Spartacus revolt in Rome to the Russian Civil War and by allegorical depictions of the October Revolution. In the latter, for example, the bourgeois state was often shown as a wall which after the final struggle was 'razed to the ground', opening the way to the Commune.

All mass spectacles concluded with an obligatory singing of 'The Internationale' by actors and spectators together. Although players and audience often joined together in a parade or the like, more active participation on the part of the spectators still remained a distant goal.[17]

As both a representative of Proletkult and a member of the board of Tsentroteatr, a ministerial body above TEO, Kerzhentsev was a central figure at the Congress of Workers' and Peasants' Theatre in December 1919. Another prominent delegate was the prophet of ritual theatre, Vyacheslav Ivanov.

A great many non-Communist cultural personalities had found employment at TEO's Petrograd and Moscow offices, but it would be erroneous to conclude that the Theatre Section therefore functioned mainly as a refuge for them. The impact of symbolist and post-symbolist ideas on the early Soviet theatre was great. Ivanov, at least, was respected as a great innovator, and his ideas wielded considerable influence on the post-revolutionary theatrical debate.[18] At the First All-Russian Congress of Popular Enlightenment in early May 1919 Ivanov presented his thesis on 'organising the creative forces of the popular collective in the theatre'. As ten years previously, his idea was that of a people's collective theatre as an expression of

> . . . the victory of the new, organic culture over that of yesterday, which was characterised by alienation between classes and individuals, by struggles, isolation and schisms among both persons and groups.[19]

It seemed to the poet that the October Revolution had made this cultural metamorphosis possible. Yet it is obvious that Ivanov, as before, regarded the *people* as the organic collective through which the great Synthesis would emerge: the proletariat is conspicuous by its absence in his thesis. The specific theatrical forms Ivanov proposed were still strikingly similar to those presented in Kerzhentsev's *The Creative Theatre* – song festivals interspersed with theatre; mass festivals expanded into great spectacles involving the active participation of everyone; outdoor theatre with monumental allegorical scenes from the past. The difference – as Tairov was quick to point out – was that, whereas Kerzhentsev had an abstract proletariat as the foundation of his theatrical revolution, Ivanov had an abstract people. What Ivanov was arguing for was the purest form of the old 'ritual' utopia, in which the theatre itself was allotted a central rôle as the unifying force of society.

We can get some idea of how topical pre-revolutionary theories were during these years from the fact that even Nietzsche's opposition between the Apollonian and the Dionysian was transferred to the discussion of socialist theatrical policy. The traditional theatre was condemned in one debate as 'Apollonian passivity', while the proletarian mass theatre, which was regarded as an 'immediate transformation of life' rather than art, was hailed as the 'bearer of the Dionysian principle'.[20]

Yet another example of the peculiar constellations that appeared in theatrical policy during the Civil War is the commission given to Yevreinov, the apologist for individualism and aesthetic play, to direct *The Storming of the Winter Palace* in Petrograd on the third anniversary of the October Revolution in 1920. The real heroes in this production, which became the most legendary of all the mass spectacles during the Civil War, were the real Winter Palace and the real masses. Yevreinov had never been closer to realising his dream of 'theatricalising life'. With at least 8000 participants – equipped with motorcycles and armoured cars – and 100,000 spectators whose participation was merely a question of degree rather than kind, Yevreinov must have experienced the giddy sensation that the storming of the Winter Palace he was directing 'was more real than the real one'. Some of the participants may have thought differently, but for Yevreinov the *Storming* of 1920 was a victory of art over life, the triumph of theatricality over reality.[21]

When War Communism was abandoned in 1921, the huge mass spectacles – the closest to reality the dream of the ritual people's theatre had ever come in Soviet Russia – disappeared along with it. During the next few years the central problems within the radical theatre concerned the function of the theatre in traditional theatre buildings, the question of professionalism versus amateurism, and the 'representative auditorium'. The theatre of the Revolution, in other words, was followed by the revolution of the Theatre.[22]

Chapter 7

Theatre Constructivism

Meyerhold and the rationalisation of theatre

On the third anniversary of the Revolution, 7 November 1920, the same day that Yevreinov directed his mass spectacle *Storming of the Winter Palace* in Petrograd, Meyerhold opened at the RSFSR Theatre No. 1 in Moscow. Together with his assistant Valery Bebutov and a newly organised troupe, he commemorated the holiday with the staging of the Belgian symbolist Verhaeren's revolutionary drama *The Dawn (Les Aubes)*.[1]

We have seen that the Revolution and Civil War had breathed new life into the notion of the *representative auditorium*. Now, if ever, Wagner's ideal of the ancient Greek 'people's theatre' was to become reality: the audience that had been divided for so long was again to become *whole*, a representative for the entire collective. And through the audience the theatre would speak to the collective and stand at the centre of all society. Even if Meyerhold was sceptical toward the idea that the theatre should dissolve in a mass spectacle which erased the boundaries between spectators and actors, he was fully in sympathy with the notion of the representative auditorium. Just before the rehearsals of *The Dawn* he proclaimed enthusiastically that 'each spectator represents, as it were, a model of Soviet Russia'.[2] Thus the theatre's prospects for penetrating and influencing daily life seemed promising indeed.

Verhaeren's drama is an allegory situated in an abstract time and space. Meyerhold and his set designer Dmitriev made the decor consist of non-figurative planes in different colours with a few cubes to serve as

65

speaking platforms and the like. The producers also, however, harked back to the unifying form of the Greek theatre, introducing to bind together and comment upon the action a chorus that was partly visible in the orchestra pit between the stage and the stalls. The actors wore no make-up, and the lights in the auditorium were left on. The chorus and claques out in the auditorium urged the audience to take part in the eulogies to the revolutionary leaders. The nature of the production as a mass meeting was at its most obvious when the column representing the old order was pulled down and actors and spectators sang 'The Internationale' in unison.

Another item in this rather abstract and monumental production aroused a great sensation. On 18 November 1920 Meyerhold had the courier in Verhaeren's play read an authentic news telegram of the same day, reporting the final victory of the Red Army over the Whites. An eyewitness at the RSFSR Theatre No. 1 describes the event as follows:

> It is difficult to describe what happened in the theatre when this historic telegram was read. Such an explosion of shouts, exclamations, applause, such a universal, delighted, I would say furious, roar never was heard within the walls of a theatre. The impression was strengthened because the news of the defeat of the enemy solidly and organically fitted into the fabric of the entire show, as though supplementing it with a bright episode dictated by life itself. A greater merging of art and reality I have never seen in theatre, either before or since.[3]

Thereafter new telegrams were read at every performance of *The Dawn*.

What was interesting about Meyerhold's device of letting a messenger from revolutionary reality burst into the allegorical play, however, was hardly – as the eyewitness above would have it – that art and reality were 'united', but rather that they confronted each other *without* erasing the distinction between them. For a moment reality got the upper hand and the aesthetic function played a subordinate rôle. If the audience had been presented with a telegram from 1917 – as they were in Yevreinov's mass spectacle in Petrograd – or if they had construed the telegram as merely 'part of the play', their reaction would have been different. But here the aesthetic function in the setting, the actors' declamation, and so on, was confronted with the practical function in the telegram from the front. The telegram also, of course, acquired an aesthetic function or meaning in the allegorical play as a symbol of a universal revolutionary triumph. The interesting point is, however, that a real fact was presented that was meaningful because it was, and to an extent remained, a real fact.

Meyerhold's introduction of the news telegram in *The Dawn* raised far-reaching questions: could facts from reality be placed in an artistic context without thereby immediately changing function and becoming 'aestheticised'? Did this imply that it was possible to create an art that was neither a reproduction (of the surface of reality, as in Naturalism, or of its deeper essence, as in the Symbolist stylised theatre), nor play or ritual (as Yevreinov's 'theatre-in-life' and the mass spectacle), but at once both art and action rooted in reality?

Towards biomechanics

Besides heading the RSFSR Theatre No. 1, in the autumn of 1920 Meyerhold had also been given command of the Moscow TEO. In a series of speeches and contributions to TEO's journal *Vestnik Teatra* (*The Theatre Herald*) he advanced and defended the slogan 'October of the Theatre', that is, a revolution in the theatre that would break the hegemony of the academic institutions and pave the way for his theatre of the new society.

Meyerhold was unquestionably attracted to the idea of the mass spectacle. In the spring of 1921 he planned a gigantic open-air production outside Moscow (which never materialised, however), and *The Earth in Turmoil* (1923) was staged several times outside, once at a mass festival in honour of the Fifth Congress of the Comintern in June 1924. As in 1908, however, Meyerhold was interested above all in working with the professional theatre and the professional actor. It was the general shift toward professionalism and rationality – from 'the theatre of the revolution' to 'revolution of the theatre' – that marked the beginning of Meyerhold's new period of glory in the Russian theatre.

Even before the rehearsals of *The Dawn*, Meyerhold poked fun at the prophets of the mass spectacle, proclaiming that 'the masses' could easily be presented on stage with the help of only seven actors.[4] What was, and remained, most important to him was the skilful actor whose superior technique could captivate an entire audience. In a debate on 9 December 1920 he maintained that a new theatrical pedagogy was needed to 'create a new, strong actor possessing great pathos, an enthusiasm that can infect and transform the entire auditorium'.[5] In the autumn of 1921, when the left had been defeated, he himself had been removed from the TEO and his theatre had in reality been closed down, Meyerhold retired temporarily to pedagogical work at the new State Theatrical School, where he experimented on a new actor's method, soon to be known under the name 'biomechanics'.

The very name of the method suggested a connection with general 'production theory'. The most immediate source of the term 'biomechanics' was Alexei Gastev's controversial Taylorist programme for scientific management, which in the years after the Civil War figured prominently as a model for the theoreticians of production art.[6]

In a paper on biomechanics delivered on 12 June 1922 Meyerhold explained the relationship between his theory and the production process in the new, if as yet only outlined, society:

> Work should be made easy, congenial and uninterrupted, whilst art should be utilised by the new class not only as a means of relaxation but as something *organically vital* to the labour pattern of the worker. *We need to change not only the forms of our art but our methods too.*
> . . .
> The work of the actor in an industrial society will be regarded as a means of production vital to the proper organisation of the labour of every citizen of that society.[7]

Similar to Rodchenko and the other Constructivists at the '5 × 5 = 25' exhibition (1921), who declared that their non-figurative work was to be considered as a kind of blueprint for future everyday articles, Meyerhold thus now wanted to bestow upon what he regarded as the central element of theatre – the spatial movement of the actor – the rank of model for the production process.

Meyerhold's interest in the essentials of acting went along his whole career. He had devoted himself especially to experiments in this field in his studio on Borodin Street in St Petersburg in the years 1913–17. There, 'Doctor Dapertutto' and his students had worked to revive the tradition of *commedia dell'arte* and popular farce, the sources of European theatricality which naturalism and psychologism had forgotten. The quest for the 'basics' of theatre had led to a discovery of the possibilities, firstly, of the segmentation of scenic action into separate units or even acrobatic 'numbers' (attractions, as Eisenstein later would call them) and, secondly, of the 'grotesque' combination of the high and the low, the beautiful and the ugly, the tragic and the comic in one image. The recent trends in reflex psychology and Taylor's system for describing the minimal units of the working process now inspired Meyerhold to go further in investigating the basics of stage action.

The first results of Meyerhold's new experiments were shown in two productions in 1922, Ferdinand Crommelynck's *The Magnanimous Cuckold* and Sukhovo-Kobylin's *The Death of Tarelkin*. Significantly enough, both plays were grotesque farces with far from happy endings. The literary content of the plays was, however, overshadowed by the striking action. Meyerhold invited constructivist artists (Lyubov Popova and Varvara Stepanova, respectively) to design props, or rather acting tools, which were placed on a bare stage without any decor or curtain. During the performances the constructions were taken over by actors clad in working clothes who, with amazing acrobatic skill and rhythmical precision, demonstrated man's struggle with the inert matter of his environment. Through the strict 'biomechanical' segmentation of the actors' movements, Meyerhold achieved striking effects of synchronisation and counterpoint which left the spectators with a paradoxical feeling of lightness and comic euphoria.

Thus, in the form of joyful experiment, the actors displayed perfect control of bodies, objects and situations. The implied utopian message was that one day this skill would become the property of all; and when it did, the theatre would actually dissolve into everyday life.[8] Meyerhold's literary adviser, Ivan Aksyonov, described the utopia as follows:

The theatrical performance was to be given up in favour of a free play of workers at rest who spent part of their leisure time in a game that was perhaps improvised next to the temporarily abandoned workplace.[9]

It was thus thought that the audience, regarded as a representative of the new society as a whole ('every spectator represents a model of Soviet Russia'), would witness its own future – not, however, as a fictive 'picture of the future' for the imagination, but as an experimental demonstration. There was of course a link between the themes of the dramatic text and the superb acrobatics of the actors in *The Magnanimous Cuckold* and *The Death of Tarelkin*. But Meyerhold's primary interest now was the *tension* between the natural function of various scenic elements and their symbolic or sign function, the tension he had exploited in *The Dawn* by introducing authentic telegrams into the text of the play. The important thing now, however, was not the verbal text but something more central, namely the physical movements of the players. The dynamics, swift reflexes and acrobatic agility of Meyerhold's biomechanically trained actors did not 'depict' a superb control of the body but were in fact proof of real physical superiority. As in the circus, the movements of the performers did not *signify* difficult acts but really *were* difficult. To the same extent that the productions at Meyerhold's theatre were dominated by real and exemplarily performed actions, they pointed *out from* the theatre toward exhibition and parade, away from the theatre as a form of purely symbolic communication.[10]

Action and expressiveness

To the audience, the connection between the 'utopian' biomechanical experiments in *The Magnanimous Cuckold* and *The Death of Tarelkin* and the current tasks of Soviet society was, to put it mildly, not self-evident. As we have already seen, utilitarian production aesthetics, which called non-figurative compositions 'constructions' and the biomechanical acting technique 'a laboratory of the new man', functioned to a great extent as a *legitimating theory*. The avant-garde wanted to give its continued investigation of the basic elements of every art form – the word, the form, the movement, and so on 'as such' – a socially useful function (or at least the illusion thereof). Even if the declarations of production aesthetics were taken at face value, however, the actual social application of artistic experiments was deferred to a diffuse utopian future of material abundance in which the boundaries between intellectual and manual labour would be erased; in other words, to the classless communist society.

This, then, was abstract production art – the 'maximum programme' of the doctrine. At the same time, a part of the avant-garde developed the tactical 'minimum programme' of agitational art in the form of posters, political poetry, advertisements, and so on. Here the mission of the artist was broadened from the organisation of artistic material in the narrow sense to include *organisation of the receiver*, of the consciousness of the audience and the collective. In the theatre that nourished the myth of the representative auditorium this opened up new possibilities for organising and influencing society as a whole.

In the first constructivist productions Meyerhold had laid emphasis on the organisation of the *scenic* material. Now the director and ensemble were confronted with the task of presenting a performance with an immediate and topical political function. On 23 February 1923, the fifth anniversary of the founding of the Red Army, the theatre was to stage a 'political revue' where not only the stage but also the audience were to become material to be 'moulded' by all means available in the arsenal of sophisticated theatrical technique.

The poet Sergey Tretyakov, who had recently joined the theatre as an expert on verbal expression, was assigned the task of transforming the Belgian playwright Marcel Martinet's *La Nuit*, a melodrama dealing with an army mutiny in an anonymous kingdom, into an effective scenario for a political agitational play. A resolute 'text montage' was used to delete tedious passages in the dialogue, sharpen the intrigue, and underscore the comic depiction of the authorities and the pathos of the heroic scenes of the mutiny. The new composition was renamed *The Earth in Turmoil*. At least as important as the thematic reworking, however, was the strictly rational reorganisation of the linguistic expression plane of the text. The technical expertise of Futurism proved useful, not to demonstrate a more or less utopian linguistic freedom, however, but to affect the spectator *here and now* as effectively as possible. Tretyakov declared that in the production, which aimed at *'influencing the audience directly'*, we have concentrated on a precise rendering of the text and on its phonetic expressiveness, which has required that attention be shifted from the rhythmical aspect (the vowels) to the articulatory and onomatopoetic (the consonants)'.[11]

The tendency to utilise the rationality organised scenic material for 'direct agitation' of the spectator was most of all apparent in the set design, again by Lyubov Popova. Instead of the abstract props used in earlier experimental performances, real machine guns, motorcycles and other objects were brought on stage. Meyerhold explained why:

> With that goal in view, the assembler [the director] attempts to achieve not an aesthetic effect, but an effect that is indistinguishable from what the spectator experiences in real phenomena such as manoeuvres, parades, street demonstrations, etc. Costumes and things (great and small) are exactly as in reality; their nature as products is in the centre – no decorative embellishments, no theatrical tricks.[12]

Out with theatrical mysticism, in with real things, real effective movements, real actions! It would appear that the avant-garde dream of abolishing the closed work of art and integrating art with daily life had very nearly come true.

We saw in the preceding section that, as soon as an everyday object is introduced onto the stage, it is regarded differently: a sign function is expected, a secondary function in addition to the practical, everyday one. Meyerhold was of course aware of the fact, for otherwise he would not have brought things that worked 'exactly as in reality' into the theatre. The actors did not drill on stage to become good soldiers, and the machine guns did not rattle away in order to kill anyone. They were there to express and signify something. Just as the leaps and somersaults of the actors in *The Magnanimous Cuckold* were at once real and difficult and signified abstract properties such as 'self-control', 'swiftness', and 'supremacy over things', the uniforms, formations and munitions were there to signify the principle of military coordination, or, as Tretyakov even put it, 'the military formation as the most rational form for the organisation of the human collective'. The heavy, coordinated objects on Meyerhold's stage acquired an agitational function because they were regarded as *expressive*, and not just everyday objects.

The pursuit of expressiveness in *The Earth in Turmoil* – from the crowd scenes down to the phonetic structure of the individual lines – was determined by the orientation of the agitational performance toward the spectator. How most effectively to influence and 'organise' the audience was currently the most important task confronting the theatre. Tretyakov declared the mission of the revolutionary theatre in relation to the audience to be 'the invention of superior forms for the organisation of the crowd into a coordinated collective'.[13]

Intensifying the expressive power of the material in *The Earth in Turmoil* was merely a beginning. If the task of the theatre was to transform the audience from a 'crowd' into a 'collective', the question of the function of the audience, that is, the role of the receiver in the act of communication that the theatrical performance constitutes, would have to be posed much more precisely. This was one of the most important points in Tretyakov's collaboration in 1923–4 with Meyerhold's student Sergey Eisenstein. Their experiments and discussions in the Moscow Proletkult Theatre, like the above-mentioned productions at Meyerhold's theatre, should be viewed in the context of the doctrine of production art as applied to theatre.

'The factory for the new man'

The theory of production art was, as we have seen, an attempt to give the development towards non-figurativism a positive sociological attribute. The authors of the theory, Brik and Arvatov, claimed to have discovered and formulated universally applicable laws of artistic evolution in the industrialised transitional society (cf. pp. 23–6 above). It was only natural that the theatre, the most public art form, should have held a special attraction for the advocates of production art.

Boris Arvatov developed his concept of the evolution of theatre in a series of articles in 1922–5, the first of which bore the programmatic title

'Theatre as Production'. Its basic argument, which Arvatov in essence merely repeated later with great perserverance, was a variant of overall production aesthetics. In capitalist society, the critic stated, theatre (like all art) was a *compensatory sphere* in which the actors and the bourgeois audience encountered in the form of illusion a beauty and a possibility of creation that did not exist outside, in society. In the socialist society now being built, by contrast, there would no longer be any need for this ideological pseudo-world. Attempts to breathe life into the theatre by binding together actor and spectator in a common 'ritual' play, even if this were done under proletarian slogans, were categorically rejected by Arvatov.

The theory of production art maintained that the revolution and the proletariat – led by artists regarded as 'producers' – would create an art that did not reflect but actively *organised* reality. For the theatre this meant that the skills of the producer and the actor would become a part of the everyday world of the common citizen:

> The future proletarian theatre will become a platform for the creative forms of reality; it will develop life-styles and human models; it will be transformed into a single great laboratory for the new public life, and will take for its materials every manner of social function.
>
> The theatre as production, the theatre as a factory for the skilled man – this is what will sooner or later be inscribed on the banner of the working class.[14]

What the future 'production theatre' would look like was not clearly described by Arvatov, who tended to limit himself to catch-phrases such as the above. He was, however, more specific as to *which way* it was to develop. It would walk 'over the dead body of the earlier theatre', that is, it would be effected through the avant-garde's liberation of the language of form from any illustrative, mimetic function and through a transformation of previous scales of values. In futurist 'eccentrism' and in Meyerhold's biomechanics Arvatov perceived what he called a 'proletarianisation' of theatrical devices themselves. By this he meant an evolution away from the illusions of naturalism toward a subordination of scenic elements to the general principles of modern art production (Cubism) that, again, were seen as analogous to the new society's universal forms of organisation.

The Russian avant-garde had conducted a few theatrical experiments before the war, principally Mayakovsky's tragedy *Vladimir Mayakovsky* and Kruchenykh's *Victory over the Sun*, both of which were staged in St

Petersburg during the Futurists' heyday in 1913. Otherwise their interest
in the theatre had perhaps been most clearly expressed in their famous
carnivalesque tour of 1913–14 and in other similar appearances, and it
was not until after the Revolution that Futurism entered the theatre in
earnest. Between 1919 and 1923 a wave of burlesque music-hall, acrobatics, slapstick and buffoonery swept through the small theatres of
Petrograd and Moscow. This eccentrism, which should be viewed as a
reaction against both the realism of the academic theatres and the
highflown monumental spectacles of the Civil War years, was directly
connected with Futurism and Dadaism in Western Europe.[15]

Eccentrism was a short-lived vogue in Russia that was codified above
all in films such as Kuleshov's *The Extraordinary Adventures of Mr
West in the Land of the Bolsheviks* and Kozintsev and Trauberg's *The
Adventures of Oktyabrina* (both 1924). As a source of inspiration and
ideas for the film, theatre and political revue of the 1920s, however, it
was very significant. Meyerhold himself – who in a sense had already
sponsored the trend before the Revolution through his interest in *commedia
dell'arte* and *balagan* (the Russian marketplace theatre) – both defended
and used 'eccentric' devices. Shortly before the première of the second
version of Mayakovsky's *Mystery-Bouffe* (1921) he had referred explicitly to a manifesto by Marinetti in which the Italian Futurist recommended performing plays backwards, pouring glue on the seats, strew-
ing sneezing powder over the audience, arranging fires and fistfights in
the auditorium, and organising sports events outside the theatre during
the intermission – 'all to the glory of speed and dynamism'.[16] *Mystery-
Bouffe* included an act by the clown Lazarenko, whom Meyerhold had
walking a tightrope on stage. The subsequent biomechanical performances were full of acrobatics and fast slapstick; despite their strict discipline, both *The Magnanimous Cuckold* and *The Death of Tarelkin*, after
all, were basically comedies with plenty of grotesque farce.

Futurist eccentrism had important consequences for the view of the
theatre as a sign system. Dividing the action on stage into a series of
more or less independent 'numbers' meant that it could no longer be
regarded as even an extremely 'conventional' reflection of events outside the theatre. What remained was the autonomous, 'non-figurative'
scenic action. As Arvatov put it, 'the theatrical event is its own subject'.

This 'non-figurative' tendency also had another side that has already
been discussed in connection with Meyerhold's biomechanical performances. On stage it is ordinarily of no consequence whether a suitcase
lifted by an actor weighs 4 or 40 pounds – the important thing is whether
his movements signify 'carrying a heavy bag'; the practical function,

that is, 'difficulty', is completely overshadowed by the symbolic or sign function. But in Meyerhold's biomechanical productions the balance between the two functions sometimes shifted suddenly, and the attention of the audience was directed toward the players' skill and work on stage instead of solely toward what they might be illustrating.

Besides Meyerhold's theatre, Arvatov called attention to another experimental theatre that was not only involved with 'proletarianising forms' but also had a positive programme based on the principles of production art. This was the Moscow Proletkult's First Workers' Theatre, which from the spring of 1922 was headed by Arvatov himself and by Sergey Eisenstein. Arvatov pointed out two lines of activity for the theatre, in accordance with the division in the theory of production art between a 'minimum programme' (agitational art) and a 'maximum programme' (production art proper). The closest the latter came to realisation seems to have been the curriculum Eisenstein and Arvatov drew up for the Moscow Proletkult 'director's workshop'. Subjects taught included the following:

> theoretical: scientific labour management, movement rationalisation in everyday life, psychotechnique, theory of monumental composition; practical (the 'theatricalisation' but not the aestheticising of the everyday): experimental laboratory of kinetic constructions (individual and collective) on the basis of an elaborate three-dimensional plan, construction of such plans, improvised kinetic constructions (conference, banquet, tribunal, meeting, mass meeting, theatre auditorium, athletic exhibitions and competitions, club gatherings, foyers, public lunchrooms, popular festivals, marches, carnivals, funerals, parades, demonstrations, rallies, election campaigns, strikes, factory work, etc., etc.).[17]

Above we have schematised three types of ideal relationship between stage and auditorium: 'naturalism', 'stylised theatre', and 'ritual theatre'. Having analysed Meyerhold's experiments and Arvatov's conceptions, important points of which coincide, we can now set up a fourth type, 'constructivism', with the following distinctive features:

1. *Footlights eliminated*. Meyerhold's biomechanical performances did not play with the footlights to emphasise theatricality (as in the 'stylised theatre'). The footlights are eliminated as the stage opens out into the auditorium and the theatre becomes exhibition, parade, demonstration of 'the skilled individual'.

2. *Incongruence* between stage and auditorium. The stage shows

and tests that which is not yet possible in real life. Even the strict rationality of the military organisation in *The Earth in Turmoil* was more utopia than reality in 1923.

    3. *Direction out from* the world of the stage. What is shown on stage is the future of the spectators, but it is not an imagined 'picture of the future', rather it is an experiment to be emulated in life outside the theatre. To the same extent that the stage is dominated by *real*, model actions (e.g. difficult acrobatic stunts) instead of *signs* for actions, the theatrical function tends to recede and the theatre becomes exhibition, parade, and so on. We can add a figure to our diagram:

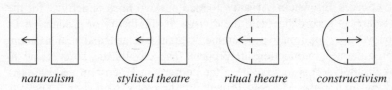

   naturalism   *stylised theatre*   *ritual theatre*   *constructivism*

Chapter 8

The Theatre of Attractions

The circus as laboratory

Toward the end of 1922 Meyerhold's student Sergey Eisenstein had
assumed the artistic direction of the First Workers' Theatre of the Moscow Proletkult. Shortly before presenting his first independent production, the young director published the manifesto 'The Montage of Attractions', in which he said that:

> The spectator himself constitutes the basic material of the theatre; the
> objective of every utilitarian theatre . . . is to guide the spectator in the
> desired direction (frame of mind).[1]

Thus the view of *the audience as material* was central from the outset.
We have already encountered it in our analysis of *The Earth in Turmoil*.
Unlike the master improviser Meyerhold, however, who worked intuitively and unsystematically, the leaders of the little Proletkult Theatre
aspired to develop a theory for transforming the audience, as Tretyakov
put it, from a 'crowd' into a 'coordinated collective'.

Sergey Eisenstein's early career in the theatre was long shrouded in
obscurity. In recent years, however, it has become clear that the previous
lack of information was not coincidental, the main explanation being
that all of Eisenstein's theatrical work was intimately connected with
Vsevolod Meyerhold and Sergey Tretyakov, both victims of the Terror
in 1937–9 and thus for many years unmentionable in the Soviet Union.[2]

When the future film director took over the Moscow Proletkult stage

77

Sergei Eisenstein
The Montage of Attractions

For the production of A. N. Ostrovsky's *Enough Stupidity in Every Wiseman* at the Proletkult Theatre in Moscow

I. THE THEATRICAL LINE OF THE PROLETKULT

In a few words. The theatrical programme of the Proletkult does not involve the 'utilisation of the values of the past' or the 'invention of new forms of theatre' but the abolition of the very institution of theatre as such, replacing it with a showplace for achievements in the theatre or with an instrument for raising the *standard of training of the masses in their day-to-day life*. The real task of the scientific section of the Proletkult in the field of the theatre is to organise theatre studios and to work out a scientific system for raising this standard.

All the rest that is being done is 'provisional'; to fulfil secondary, not basic, aims of the Proletkult. The 'provisional' runs along two lines under the general heading of revolutionary content.

1. *Representational-narrative theatre* (static, real-life – the right wing): *The Dawn of Proletkult, Lena*, and a series of not fully realised productions of the same type – this being the direction of the former Workers' Theatre with the Central Committee of Proletkult.

2. *Agit-attraction theatre* (dynamic and eccentric – the left wing): the direction promoted by me in collaboration with Boris Arvatov, chiefly for the work of the Touring Troupe of the Moscow Proletkult. . . .

II. THE MONTAGE OF ATTRACTIONS

Since this concept is being used for the first time, it requires some explanation.

The spectator himself constitutes the basic material of the theatre; the objective of every utilitarian theatre (agit, poster, health education, etc.) is to guide the spectator in the desired direction (frame of mind). The means of achieving this are all the component parts of the theatrical apparatus, ([the actor] Ostuzhev's 'chatter' as much as the colour of the prima donna's tights, a stroke on the kettledrum as much as a soliloquy of Romeo, the cricket on the hearth no less than a salvo under the seats of the spectators); in all their heterogeneity, all the component parts of the theatrical apparatus are reduced to a single unit – thereby justifying their presence – by being attractions.

An attraction (in relation to the theatre) is any aggressive aspect of the theatre; that is, any element of the theatre that subjects the spectator to emotional or psychological impact, experimentally regulated and mathematically calculated to produce in him certain emotional shocks which, when placed in their proper sequence within the totality of the production, become the only means that enable the spectator to perceive the ideological side of what is being demonstrated – the ultimate ideological conclusion. (The means of cognition – 'through the living play of passions' – apply specifically to the theatre.)

Sensual and psychological, of course, are to be understood in the sense of immediate reality, in the way these are handled, for example, by the Grand Guignol theatre: gouging out eyes or cutting off arms and legs on the stage – or a character on stage participating by telephone in a ghastly event ten miles away; of the plight of a drunkard who senses his approaching death, and whose cries for help are taken as delirium tremens – not in terms of the development of psychological problems where the attraction is already the theme of the play itself – a theme that exists and functions even outside the play's action provided that it is sufficiently topical. (This is an error into which agit-theatres fall, satisfied with only this kind of attraction in their productions.)

On the formal level, by an attraction I mean an independent and primary element in the construction of a performance – a molecular (that is, compound) unit of effectiveness in theatre and of theatre in general. It is fully analogous to Grosz's 'storehouse of images' or Rodchenko's 'elements of photo-illustrations'. . . .

A genuinely new approach radically changes the possibilities in the principles of building a 'construction that has impact' (the performance as a whole), instead of a static 'reflection' of a given event necessary for the theme, and of the possibility of its resolution solely through effects logically connected with such an event. A new method emerges – free montage of arbitrarily selected independent (also outside the given composition and the plot links of the characters) effects (attractions) but with a view to establishing a certain final thematic effect – montage of attractions.

The way of completely freeing the theatre from the weight of the 'illusory imitativeness' and 'representationality' which up until now has been definitive, inevitable, and solely possible, is through a transition to montage of 'workable artifices'. At the same time, this allows interweaving into the montage whole 'representational segments' and connected plot lines of action, no longer as something self-contained and all-determining, but as an immediately effective attraction consciously selected for a given purpose. The sole basis of such a performance does not lie in 'the discovery of the playwright's intention', 'the correct interpretation of the author', 'the true reflection of the period', etc., but only in attractions and a system of attractions. Any director who has become a skilled hand due to a natural flair has intuitively used an attraction in some way or other, but, of course, not in terms of a montage or construction but 'in a harmonious composition', at any rate (hence even the jargon – 'effective curtain', 'rich exit', 'good stunt', etc.). But what is significant is that what was done was only in the framework of logical plot probability ('warranted' by the play) and chiefly unconsciously, in pursuit of something completely different (something that was not in what was calculated 'in the beginning'). In terms of working out a system for constructing a performance, there remains only to transfer the centre of attention to what is proper, what was previously considered secondary and ornamental, but what actually is the basic guide for the production's nonconforming intentions and, without becoming logically bound by real life and traditional literary piety, *to establish the given approach as the production method* (the work of the Proletkult workshops from the fall of 1922).

From *Lef*, No. 2 (1923)

---

he had studied for a year at Meyerhold's school and worked as an assistant on *The Death of Tarelkin*. Even before this, at the age of 23 in the spring of 1921, he had aroused attention as the set designer and co-director of the production of *The Mexican* (scenario by Arvatov, based on a story by Jack London) at the Proletkult Theatre, a work that had a liberal sprinkling of music-hall and eccentrism, with a 'genuine' boxing match on an arena stage in the auditorium, and so on.

Eisenstein's first production as leader and director at the Proletkult Theatre was also quite within the trend of futurist eccentrism. Evidently with the purpose of shocking the traditionalist audience and critics, he chose to commemorate the nineteenth-century classic Alexander

Ostrovsky's centennial with an 'adaptation' which left little of the well-known comedy *Enough Stupidity in Every Wiseman* untouched. One possible model was the FEKS 'electrification of Gogol' recently presented in Petrograd, but the influence of Marinetti's music-hall manifesto had made itself felt on all eccentric ventures.[3]

To adapt Ostrovsky's play as the scenario of an eccentrist revue Eisenstein turned to Tretyakov, whose literary skill and radical temperament he knew from Meyerhold's theatre. Tretyakov's text became in reality a new play, although the intrigue and some of the lines of the original were retained. Ostrovsky's spatial and temporal indications were completely changed: the rogue Glumov became a White émigré of 1923 who nestled himself into the salons of international reaction in Paris; the gullible Mamayev became the Kadet leader Milyukov, Krutitsky appeared as the French general Joffe, and so on. The lines that were retained from the original text were supplied with contemporary political references and with clownish and frivolous puns.

Tretyakov's text montage bearing the abbreviated title *Mudrets* (*Wiseman*) was thus a futuristic murder of an old standby in the bourgeois theatrical repertory. Eisenstein's intention, however, was not only to clown around with a classic. The text as such, parodic or not, played a subordinate rôle in the production, which opened at the Proletkult Theatre on 26 April 1923. Tretyakov's scenario served as a platform to launch a pyrotechnical display of eccentrist farce and circus tricks. The Proletkult Theatre auditorium had been transformed into a kind of arena with a round riding-track in the middle, and the props consisted of things such as horizontal bars, pedestals, a tightrope, and so on. The intrepid young actors – and behind them the even younger but omnipotent director – presented a chain of acrobatic and comical numbers that were only at times linked together by the text.

In his manifesto Eisenstein had introduced the term 'attraction' to designate the minimal unit of a performance, by which he meant any strong sensual or psychological shock on the spectator through which the director structures the play. Although the term was new in the theatrical context (it was borrowed from the circus), Eisenstein maintained that the phenomenon itself was old. 'Attractions' included an actor's diction and the colour of the prima donna's tights, Romeo's monologue as well as firecrackers underneath the spectators' seats. Whereas attractions were earlier used as a means of mimetic, realistic illustration, the theatre Eisenstein wanted to develop was based on the *'free montage of arbitrarily selected independent . . . effects (attractions)'*.

What was new in Eisenstein's manifesto concerned not so much the *means* employed by the theatre as its *goal*. As we have already seen, at the centre of his attention was a radical view of the spectator as 'the basic material of the theatre to be guided in the desired direction'. The powerful effects or attractions of the theatre were ultimately intended to subject the audience to 'certain emotional shocks' that would in turn lead it to draw the 'ideological conclusion' of the performance. Precisely what this conclusion was in *The Wiseman* – apart from the brutal and comical removal of Ostrovsky from the pedestal upon which he had just been raised by Lunacharsky and other guardians of tradition – probably remained unclear to the amused spectators who flocked to see what immediately became a *succès de scandale*.

Eisenstein declared in the introduction to this manifesto that his real purpose was

the abolition of the very institution of theatre as such, the replacement of it by a showplace for achievements in the theatre or by an instrument for raising the *standard of training of the masses in their day-to-day life*.

Everything but this utopian 'factory for the skilled man' was to be regarded as a provisional compromise. Such was also the zany comedy in *The Wiseman*. The play was criticised by the Proletkult political leadership as being formalistic, and it was allowed to be presented only with the designation 'experimental performance'. Like Meyerhold with *The Earth in Turmoil*, Eisenstein subsequently attempted to 'correct' his course by applying what he had learned to make the agitational play conform to the 'minimum programme' of production art theory.

From sign to action

Thus the Proletkult Theatre needed a play with a clear thematic link to the reality of the day. Tretyakov's *Do You Hear, Moscow?!* was written in response to that need and opened on 7 November 1923, the sixth anniversary of the revolution.[4] Its theme was the expected proletarian revolution in Germany. The play is set in a Bavarian industrial town owned and run by a Count Stahl (*sic*). Economic crisis has aroused 'unrest' among the workers, and to calm them, that same 7 November the Count organises a mass spectacle that includes the unveiling of a monument to his forebear, the 'Iron Count'. Secretly and despite the police terror, the Communist workers are simultaneously organising a demonstration. The townspeople gather at the marketplace for their bread and entertainment as the Count and his retinue look on. The court poet begins a pantomime telling how the old Iron Count created harmony between rulers and subjects in his day. But just as the rebellious mountain dwellers in the play are about to lay down their arms, they aim them instead at Count Stahl, and the covering falls from the monument to his predecessor to reveal – a giant portrait of Lenin. Led by the Communists disguised as actors, the crowd attacks the Count and his retinue to cries of 'Bread! Jobs! Socialism!' The Communist Hugo rushes up to the edge of the stage and shouts to the audience at the Proletkult Theatre: 'Do you hear, Moscow?!' Tretyakov's stage directions continue: *'Unanimous reply from the auditorium: "Yes, I hear!"'*

Although small in format and simplistic in theme, Tretyakov's play is rather intricately structured. The entire play is built on two opposing conspiracies – the counter-revolution of the Count and the uprising of the workers. To draw interest to the workers, their conspiracy is *partly hidden* from the audience, whereas the fascistic intrigues of the Count are completely in the open. So far, however, Tretyakov is operating with melodramatic clichés. Of greater interest are the dénouement of the play and the way in which it affects the relationship between stage and auditorium.

In the dénouement of *Do You Hear, Moscow?!* one semiotic layer after another is 'peeled away', until the audience is finally confronted with immediate reality. It is possible to discern at least four such layers possessing an increasing degree of reality and a correspondingly decreasing sign function:

(1)   the *false* unity in the Count's pantomime (play within the play);
(2)   the *genuine* (performed) unity between the (play's) German revolutionaries;
(3)   the *overarching* unity between (the actor playing) the German Communist on stage and the audience in the auditorium;
(4)   the reply of the audience 'Yes, I hear!' leads out of the fiction and into the *real* unity among the spectators at the Proletkult Theatre, joining with the actors in singing 'The Internationale' in support of the German revolution (and thereby, ultimately, uniting with their class brethren in Germany).

Thus the very structure of the play successively leads the audience out of the 'illusory' theatrical sign world that is realised at its purest in the Count's counter-revolutionary play, and into the world of (proposed) immediate political action.[5]

The theatre as 'processing of the spectator'

The 'theatre of attractions', then, was a form of constructivist or 'production' theatre that paid special attention to the spectator. In the first three of our schematicised types of theatre presented above the spectator's role is *active*: in naturalism it involves identification; in the stylised theatre it is interpretative, and in the ritual theatre it is participatory. In the fourth type, constructivism, the spectators, paradoxically, seem to be *passive*. They are regarded as the centre of the theatre, but only as material, as an object. To some extent, however, the contradiction is only an apparent one, since the theatre aspires to 'mould' the spectators to make them better prepared to act; the action itself belongs to the sphere of practical reality outside the theatre. Still, the contradiction remains that in the extremely utilitarian and rational 'production theatre' it is only the artists – the director and the actors – who are responsible for the rational, whereas the spectators do not cease being objects and become rational subjects until they find themselves outside the receiver situation.

The notion of the spectator in the 'theatre of attractions' appears to have emerged from Eisenstein's and Tretyakov's collaborative efforts. Their account of new trends in physical training ('Expressive Movement') and a number of journalistic articles by Tretyakov elaborated their view of the relationship between theatre and audience.

The 'theatre of attractions', Tretyakov states in one article, is predicated upon the tendencies of all modern art (echoes of Brik and Arvatov are easily discernible) to free itself from every psychological or representational intent and to focus instead on material and form: cubism in painting, the 'autonomous word' of futurism, the montage of physical movements in biomechanism. The fact that the advocates of production art attempt to give art a utilitarian function in the new society should not be taken to mean a retreat to the earlier enslavement of art by theme. The course is 'from form to social application, not the other way around'. As in other branches of art, the theatre's utilitarian function involves finding applications for the artist's autonomously developed knowledge of material and form (often through *postulating* its social applicability).

According to Tretyakov, the theatre of attractions is primarily a theatre that seeks to influence the emotions. Referring to Eisenstein, he defines an 'attraction' as 'any calculated impact on the feelings of the spectator'. The method of the theatre of attractions is to seize and 'charge' the spectator. Or, as Tretyakov categorically put it: 'The theatrical show is replaced by the theatrical blow, by the immediate processing of the audience.' To achieve this 'immediate processing', however, a rational method is needed. One must 'find ways to estimate the effects, the emotional tension, that the theatre seeks to evoke in the audience'.[6]

Eisenstein later declared that if he had been better acquainted with Pavlov's psychology of conditioning at the time the theatre of attractions was developed, he would have called it 'the theory of artistic stimuli'.[7] If Pavlov's theory was of no consequence to the directors at the Proletkult Theatre, however, they were strongly influenced by another Russian neurologist and psychiatrist, Vladimir Bekhterev, and his notion of 'collective reflexes'. According to Bekhterev, the individual's conditioned reflexes were not only affected by society, but also became, through imitation, a part of the collective experience. The actions and reactions of the collective could therefore be traced back to 'collective or social reflexes', which were the object of study of so-called collective reflexology.

Bekhterev's concept of 'collective experience' coincided with Bogdanov's collectivistic epistemology.[8] In practice this could evolve into a pure class psychology, since according to Bogdanov's interpreters in Proletkult, at least, 'the collective' was not a universal notion but referred to specific social classes.

Collective reflexology was a convenient theory for Eisenstein and Tretyakov, for it seemed to provide the needed guarantee that attractions or 'artistic stimuli' would evoke adequate reactions in the audience. In 1925, by which time Eisenstein was involved with the cinema but was still promoting the montage of attractions, he would express himself on this point even more clearly than had Tretyakov. The goal of the director's choice of stimuli was 'to charge the battle reflexes of the audience, i.e. a raising of the potential class tone'. A condition for the given stimuli to achieve the desired effect was

> the correct evaluation of their inevitably class-based effectiveness: i.e. a particular stimulant is capable of provoking a particular reaction (effect) only from an audience of a particular class character.[9]

In the rational and mechanical notion of the audience that Eisenstein is formulating here with reference to his first film *The Strike*, the consciousness of the audience resembles the column of mercury in a thermometer – if it is simply 'heated' sufficiently by strong and well-aimed stimuli, it will automatically rise.

Here we have come a long way from Wagner's utopian people's

theatre of great cathartic spectacles in which the aesthetic experience was both to express and reinforce the unity of the collective. The myth of the unity of the audience is there, nevertheless, although its basis has been transposed from ritual to class psychology.

As we saw above, the ideology of the people's theatre was based on the dream of unity between stage and auditorium, an auditorium that was regarded not as holding a particular audience but as representative of the collective as a whole. When Meyerhold staged Verhaeren's *The Dawn* in 1920 he looked upon each spectator as a 'model of Soviet Russia'; when his theatre addressed its spectators one could imagine it addressing the Soviet people as a whole.

In the evolution of the constructivist theatre, and especially in the agitational play, the idea of 'rational organisation' was broadened. Now the audience as well was included as 'material', which in Eisenstein's theatre of attractions finally became 'the basic material'. To be effective, however, this organisation required not only the proper methods but also an adequate material, and this last point brought up the question of the class composition of the audience. For the Proletkult Theatre's barrage of 'attractions' or stimuli to produce the desired political and ideological responses, what was ultimately needed were the correct 'collective reflexes'; that is, the audience had to have at least a potentially pure proletarian class consciousness.[10]

Theatre at the factory

After the political farce *The Wiseman* and the agitational melodrama *Do You Hear, Moscow?!*, in *The Gas Masks* the Proletkult Theatre turned to a theme grounded in contemporary Soviet reality. Tretyakov's idea for this play came from a news item in *Pravda* describing an incident in which gas-plant workers had taken things into their own hands and, without masks, had combated a leak in the main pipe at the factory. The subject, of course, conformed exactly with Proletkult's view that the working class was its own organiser and that the labour process evolved through collective experience. But if an event were taken from reality and presented on a theatre stage, would it not thereby be transformed into a naturalistic *picture* of reality that invited the spectator to identify with the 'illusory' sign world of the stage in a way that was completely rejected by constructivist aesthetics? The problem was obvious.

The aesthetics of realism is based on notions of 'the probable' and 'the typical'. Probability is regarded as necessary to elicit identification and empathy from the receiver, whereas the typical is needed if the depicted world is to be experienced as designating more than the individual case. According to the production aesthetics of the 1920s, however, art, or in this case the theatre, was either 'direct agitation' (emotional influence) or the demonstration of rational 'prototypes of labour processes' (intellectual influence). Attempting to write a play on a subject taken from contemporary life may appear to be a total retreat from these anti-realistic positions. The retreat was relative, however, and it was also given a theoretical sanction. In the theme of the self-sacrificing collective at the gas works Tretyakov believed he could unite the 'agitational' and the 'demonstrative' functions. What he wanted to show was not 'the typical' but the striking, the extraordinary, the future in the present – not a 'believable' yet actually fictive, ideological picture, but a remarkable fact from daily life presented as a model or example.

A second problem, however, concerned the choice of language or conventions by which this model was to be demonstrated on stage. The chances that a staging might lead to an unwelcome 'naturalist fallacy' on the part of the spectator were still disturbing. This prompted Tretyakov to give *The Gas Masks* a special construction and led Eisenstein as director to design the production in a particular way.

Tretyakov made his play about the accident at the gas works and the workers' struggle for their factory into a *melodrama*. All the writer's plays in fact contain a melodramatic element that manifests itself in sudden sensational turns in the plot. In *The Earth in Turmoil* and *Do You Hear, Moscow?!* as in the later *Roar, China!* it is the social conflicts that motivate violent swings in the action and the black-and-white division of characters into two opposing camps. But there was also an element of futurist 'laying bare' of the plot construction in Tretyakov's preoccupation with the extremely conventionalised genre of melodrama. When the material of reality in *The Gas Masks* had been transformed into a sufficiently concentrated and charged text that would not be confused with realist 'mirroring', Eisenstein in turn set about confronting this text with reality.

The theatre of attractions assumed that the audience had a clear class composition. As a matter of fact, the audience at the Proletkult Theatre had been mixed, containing a substantial number of students and intellectuals; it was considered positive that the spectators of *Do You Hear, Moscow?!* had been 50 per cent white-collar, 40 per cent workers, and only 10 per cent pure NEP bourgeois. Now such 'defects' in the class composition of the audience were to be corrected. Eisenstein, however, decided not only to play *for* a proletarian audience, but also *in* a real factory, a real gas works in Moscow.

It is sometimes said that the staging of *The Gas Masks* in a genuine

factory environment represents the logical end of the constructivist theatre that viewed itself as the 'prototype' of rational social organisation
and a 'laboratory for the skilled individual'.[11] Actually, however,
Meyerhold's constructivism and biomechanics, which Eisenstein had
assimilated, did not particularly need to be demonstrated in any specific
factory, since they had to do with the *laws* governing all sorts of movement.

As in Meyerhold's *Cuckold*, the actors in *The Gas Masks* were
dressed in blue overalls. The difference was that at the gas works their
clothes were meant to designate not 'rational, effective action' but real
workers in the labour collective of the play. Special props were made of
metal and boards, background noise was created with whistles, rivet
guns, and sheet metal. The work of the collective was shown in coordinated, rhythmic movements. The climax of the performance was to come
when the coke ovens of the real gas works, which had stood silent during
the 'repairs' in the play, were lit and began to roar once again.

Here the idea that the theatre should dissolve in life seems to be
driven as far as it can go. A few critics applauded the experiment, whose
notoriety has increased with distance in time and space from the opening
night. But most of those present at the performance, including the
director himself, agreed that the staging of *The Gas Masks* at the real gas
works was actually a flop.

In reality, the 'scenery' and the actors separated. To the workers
employed at the plant the entire performance seemed odd, since the
actors did not in fact do any real work, but merely demonstrated *signs for
work*. In this unusual environment the other spectators also completely
missed the point of the play. In other words, the interior of the gas works
stubbornly refused to be transformed into a sign, to 'play along' in
Tretyakov's melodrama. The tension between the theatrical and the
practical function skilfully employed by Meyerhold in *The Earth in
Turmoil* could not be maintained. The play was 'devoured' by the
factory.[12]

In his later evaluation of the *Gas Masks* experiment Eisenstein explained that the real materials in the gas works so appealed to the director
that he was induced to leave the theatre and turn to the cinema. It is only
partly true, however, that the idea of staging *The Gas Masks* in a real gas
works was in itself an 'exit from the theatre'. As we have seen, not least
in the experience of the Russian revolutionary theatre, the physical
location of the performance is not crucial to whether or not one can
speak of 'theatre'. The specific circumstances surrounding the performance at the gas works near the Kursk Station in fact made the future film
director's 'abandonment' of the theatre into something of a myth.

Eisenstein declared before the première that the play should be presented 'only in proletarian neighbourhoods and in factories'. On 29 February 1924 *The Gas Masks* opened with a performance exclusively for the workers of the Moscow Gas Works. The first reviews followed upon closed performances for invited guests and critics on 4 and 6 March. On 11 March another staging was arranged for an audience that included *Pravda* worker correspondents. After these four performances (all of which seem to have taken place before selected audiences), the theatrical experiment at the gas works came to an end, only soon to begin a new life, this time as a legend.[13]

Besides the concrete circumstances around Eisenstein's 'exit from the theatre', his motives for the move have also come in for some mythicising. Eisenstein did not leave the theatre for the cinema because the latter was 'a step closer to reality' or the last step between the theatre and reality. He turned to the cinema because all physical things there – even a gas works, a bridge, or a landscape – are *transformed into signs*. It was not until reality was put in front of a film camera that it could be changed, under the control of the director, into an expressive 'attraction'.

Despite all efforts to control the class composition in the auditorium of the Proletkult Theatre, reactions had proved difficult to predict. Eisenstein began searching for means that could organise the 'basic material' of the spectator more reliably than had the stimuli and responses of the theatre of attractions. He wanted forms capable of creating universally valid notions that would force the spectators to think the intended thoughts and feel the intended emotions. In a word, he was looking for *symbols*. In his first films Eisenstein considered that he was not using universal symbols but was operating within the framework of a strictly class-based psychology. The road lay open, however, and as Soviet ideology in the 1930s evolved away from class struggle toward 'national' unity, the landscapes, faces and movements in Eisenstein's films acquired an increasingly universal symbolism.

Sergey Tretyakov's development away from the 'theatre of attractions' would lead in the diametrically opposite direction. Before the ways of the two friends and colleagues began to part, however, for an interesting bit of the journey they ran almost parallel.

Striking facts

In the spring of 1924 Tretyakov left Moscow and went to Peking, remaining there for a year to teach Russian literature at the university and to study Chinese culture and society. The immediate result of the trip was a series of brilliant reports in the Soviet press. Tretyakov was especially interested in the Chinese theatre, and it was largely thanks to him that the legendary actor Mei Lan-fang later toured the Soviet Union and was seen by directors such as Meyerhold, Eisenstein and Brecht.[14] For Tretyakov himself, however, the visit to China did not lead to any real re-evaluation of his earlier work in the theatre, and the main link between his Chinese experience and the agitational play *Roar, China!* that he wrote in Peking was thematic in nature.

In June 1924, in the port city Wan-hsien on the Yangtse River, an American commercial agent was killed in a fight with a Chinese coolie. The captain of the British gunboat *Cockchafer* which was there at the time decided to demonstrate the firmness of the imperial power once and for all. He demanded that the guilty man – or, if the perpetrator could not be found within 24 hours, two of his comrades – be executed, otherwise the *Cockchafer* would shell the city. The mayor yielded to this very real threat, ordered that the American be given a burial with honours, and publicly executed two innocent oarsmen.[15]

The Wan-hsien incident – revealing in a flash as it did the arrogance of Western imperialism – provided Tretyakov with the idea for a play, which, like *The Gas Masks*, was based on an actual contemporary event. Before the opening night at Meyerhold's theatre in early 1926 the author emphasised the documentary character of the work. *Roar, China!* was a 'newspaper article' presented on the stage rather than in the column of a daily. A few critics agreed with this description, maintaining that the structure of the play was entirely determined by 'reality itself', independent of dramaturgical conventions.

Closer examination, however, reveals *Roar, China!* to be a fairly consistently structured melodrama.[16] The basic pattern running through it consists of a contrasting of scenes in the Chinese harbour with scenes on the *Cockchafer*. On the one hand there is the Chinese everyday world with its poverty and squalor (only the harbour district is shown), while on the other there is the polished cleanliness and discipline of the gunboat.

The action spans exactly twenty-four hours, but the unity of time is not the only convention of the classical drama observed by Tretyakov. *Roar, China!* is divided into nine scenes, but this is in fact a surface structure that translates into a classical five-act division that better corresponds to the contents. The plot follows the traditional pattern of *introduction* (presentation of the antagonistic blocs – Chinese people/ white imperialists); *rising action* (the argument between the coolie and the agent, the latter drowns, the captain issues his ultimatum); *peripeteia* or *climax* (the mayor announces acceptance of the terms and two innocent oarsmen are selected); *falling action* (a new delegation to the *Cockchafer*, the oarsmen wait); and the *dénouement* or *catastrophe* (the execution).

Roar, China! opened at Meyerhold's theatre in Moscow on 23 January 1926. Four days earlier Eisenstein's second film *The Battleship Potemkin* had, after various delays, come to the film theatres. However, it is not the coincidence in time but rather the extensive thematic and structural similarities of the two former Proletkult colleagues' works that justify proposing a link between them. The theme of Eisenstein's well-known film is the mutiny on the battleship *Potemkin* in Odessa during the revolutionary year of 1905. Critics pointed out immediately that the work was structured on the five-act pattern of the classical drama. Eisenstein himself later noted the tension between real materials and strict principle of composition that made the film 'look like a documentary but function like a drama.[17] The film has a clear five-act structure which follows the curve *introduction – rising action – climax – falling action – dénouement*, but it differs from the tragedy in that the basic tone of the dénouement is thoroughly optimistic and triumphant (the mutinous battleship sails unscathed past the loyal squadron outside the harbour).

The theme of 'rebellion – repression', the contrasts between the spatial poles 'warship – harbour' and the classical five-act structure adequately motivate a comparison between Tretyakov's play and Eisenstein's film, but in addition to these parallels the two works are in all probability connected by external circumstances as well. In the autumn of 1924 Eisenstein had been assigned to stage an early version of Tretyakov's play entitled *Cockchafer* at the Proletkult Theatre. Shortly thereafter, however, he broke with Proletkult entirely, and the play seems to have remained untouched. In the summer of 1925, when Eisenstein had already written the script and begun shooting what would become *The Battleship Potemkin*, Tretyakov returned from China and soon joined the filming team. In October it was announced that Meyerhold's theatre would stage Tretyakov's play, which was now being called *Roar, China!*

The interesting point here is not whether Eisenstein was 'influenced' by his reading of the earlier version of Tretyakov's play or whether the final *Roar, China!* was influenced by work on the film (both seem likely). What is more worth pondering over is that the two representatives of the 'theatre of attractions' were in the space of a couple of years able to proceed from abstract futuristic montage pyrotechnics to classical five-act structures – all for the sake of agitational effects.[18]

Whereas the extremely strict form of *The Battleship Potemkin* at least held the line against the naturalistic illusion of reality that was the traditional *bête noire* of the avant-garde, Tretyakov was willing to compromise on that point as well. Citing the need for utilitarian agitational effect, in *The Gas Masks* he had partially resurrected the representational heresy. Further compromises with the theory were made in *Roar, China!*, which of course excluded any 'feedback' to reality as in the production melodrama. Since the audience in Moscow was viewing a socially and politically remote situation, it could be aroused only to sympathy, not to action.

The performance at Meyerhold's theatre, which was directed by his assistant Vasily Fyodorov rather than the Master himself, was in fact criticised for Stanislavskian naturalism and even an undisguised speculation in exoticism in its style and set design.[19] With respect to the earlier theoretical and practical ambitions of the Meyerhold theatre, *Roar, China!*, both as a play and as a performance, was a symptom of crisis. It was hugely popular nonetheless, remaining in the repertory for six years, and featured in the theatre's European tour of 1930. Soon it became the first Soviet play to enjoy an international triumph, with productions in Germany, Japan, Poland and Norway – a success which for that time can only be compared with that of *The Battleship Potemkin* in the cinema.[20]

Chapter 9

The Audience as Myth and Reality[1]

The crisis of the people's theatre utopia

As we have attempted to show, the late nineteenth-century notion of the theatre as the socially most significant art form was based on the concept of the 'representative auditorium'. The Wagnerian people's theatre utopia derived its great moral and political authority from the idea that the entire collective – the nation, the people – was sitting in the amphitheatre or was at least somehow directly represented there. When the actors addressed the audience, they were addressing the collective as a whole. And when the audience joined with the actors in the community of the theatre, this union encompassed the collective as a whole.

After the October Revolution, the notion that the entire society or working class was sitting in the auditorium endowed the theatre with an exceptional potential for influencing that society or class. All that was required was to speak as clearly and effectively as possible from the stage, and the question of the means by which the audience could be influenced or 'organised' acquired a new status. The rôle of the theatrical leader or director assumed excessive proportions; it was not for nothing that Meyerhold loved to pose in a commissar's leather coat and a military cap.

The manifestos issued by Eisenstein and Tretyakov from the Proletkult's First Workers' Theatre represent the most extreme formulation of the actor and director as sovereign experts and the spectator as

93

material. Even here, however, the spectator was not an individual spectator but a part of a collective whose reactions had to be anticipated if the theatre was to have an adequate effect not only on the audience in the auditorium but also, through class psychology, on the larger collective that it represented.

Audience responses: how? – who? – why?

The experiments at the Meyerhold theatre and the Proletkult Theatre of Eisenstein and Tretyakov had moved the problem of the audience from the shadows of implied theatrical theory to the glare of practice and debate. But there was still no empirical knowledge available. The time had come for a large-scale general discussion on the status of the audience and the possibilities for concrete audience research.

Today, more than sixty years later, the Soviet discussion of the problem of the audience of the mid-1920s is interesting from two points of view. It has a general significance as an early attempt to define the object and methods of scientific audience research. In fact, those Russian theatre specialists who participated in the debate identified and formulated problems (albeit without solving them) which theatre scholars in the West have only recently touched upon.[2] The discussion, however, was not initiated for purely theoretical reasons but because theatre workers themselves had the feeling that the concept of the political people's theatre did not work under the conditions of NEP. Thus, the discussion was a symptom of the crisis in people's theatre and the need for new approaches to the audience.[3]

In 1924, *Lef*, the journal of left art in which Eisenstein had published his 'Montage of Attractions' a year earlier, carried an article by the critic Mikhail Zagorsky pointing out the need for concrete information about the theatre audience:

> As a matter of fact, who has studied the Soviet audience during these years of revolution? Who makes up this audience? Of which class groups does it consist? What are the reactions not of this or that spectator but of these different groups to this or that performance? To the play, the staging, the theatre, the movement? To academic or 'left-wing' performances? How do a homogeneous auditorium and an auditorium with a mixed audience react to the same performance? How does this audience become differentiated in terms of class position by a revolutionary show and how does it become emotionally

unified by an academic show? What is 'comprehensible' to some and 'incomprehensible' to others? What is it in a play and a performance that lowers or wakens the activity of the audience? Or what has a subduing effect on some and a vitalising effect on others?[4]

These questions had to be raised, Zagorsky made clear, not because of the development of academic scholarship but because Soviet theatre workers talked and argued so much about the audience even though, in fact, they knew almost nothing about it.

Not to know the answers to these questions means to operate in the dark in the field of theatre work. And it seems to me that all our theatrical 'misunderstandings' spring from the fact that we do not know these answers.[5]

As an example of audience studies that would lead to answers to the questions he had raised, Zagorsky referred to his own experiments in Meyerhold's RSFSR Theatre No. 1 in the 1920–1 season. He found the widespread habit of organising discussions with the audience after the performance useless from a sociological point of view. Instead, he had organised the distribution of questionnaires, which the spectators were asked to fill in before leaving the theatre. Zagorsky regretted the fact that Meyerhold, who during the 1920–1 season had used the information given in the questionnaires for his 'orientation towards the audience', had since abandoned the method.[6]

Presenting his conclusions from the experiment of 1920–1 in his article in *Lef*, Zagorsky focused on the questionnaires he had saved from the RSFSR Theatre No. 1 about Mayakovsky's *Mystery-Bouffe*.[7] Although he had only 186 questionnaires available, Zagorsky contended that this was enough to show at least one thing: in reality the audience could not be viewed as an undifferentiated whole. Different class backgrounds had been essential to differences in the spectators' evaluation of *Mystery-Bouffe*. It was not only a matter of approving or disliking, Zagorsky asserted; workers, peasants and intellectuals had reacted positively or negatively to the performance for quite different reasons. He concluded:

There is no single spectator, neither is there a single performance. The revolutionary current turned on from the stage splits up the auditorium, organises and differentiates its positive and negative elements. And the current that is fed back from the auditorium in its turn splits up the performance, letting each group of people see on the stage what its social preconditioning allows it to see.[8]

This almost phenomenological approach to the theatre performance as an object, concretised in the interplay between the actively perceiving spectator and the stage, seems very far ahead of its time. This becomes all the clearer in the light of the discussion that was soon to be initiated by a report on the new audience research conducted by the Meyerhold theatre.

In the journal *Zhizn' iskusstva* (*Life of Art*) in the spring of 1925, Vasily Fyodorov (the assistant to Meyerhold who would soon stage *Roar, China!*) presented the results of a wide survey of audience responses in the Meyerhold theatre during the 1924–5 season.[9] The basis for the experiment was strictly utilitarian: the problem of the audience's reactions ought to be studied so that the theatre might reach its audience more effectively. To influence man in the new society, to give him new habits, a new way of thinking, yes, even 'to organise the subconsciousness of man' – all of this, according to Fyodorov, was a grandiose task which the theatre could solve better than any other art form. Thanks to the research project, Fyodorov claimed, objective knowledge about the functioning of the theatrical performance was now available,

> with the help of which we, with evidence, with documents in our hands, can disclose the total emptiness, superficiality and irresponsibility of our theatre criticism.[10]

The surveys were strictly behaviourist in spirit, the following method being employed. For every performance of a production to be studied, the theatre research group prepared a special chart on which the reactions in the auditorium during the evening could be noted. The chart had a vertical column in which was noted the concrete 'stimulus' (line, gesture, and so on) and a horizontal axis, divided into separate time units or segments of the performance. During the performance the assistant on duty was supposed to fill in a code number in the relevant square on the chart, thereby noting what kind of audience reaction was called forth by what 'stimulus' in which episode. For practical reasons the standard types of reaction had been reduced to twenty in number, ranging from 'silence' through 'laughter' or 'applause' to the extremes, 'leaving the auditorium' or 'climbing on to the stage'. The assistant was also supposed to note down on the chart general comments about the duration of the show, the audience attending (students, workers, and so on, if this was known), and whether or not there was a full house.[11]

In the material presented by Fyodorov in the *Life of Art* article, 'laughter' and 'silence' were by far the most frequent reactions, and focusing on them, comparing the sum of reactions per hour in the average performance of the productions in repertoire – Erdman's *Mandate*, Ostrovsky's *The Forest*, Fayko's *Bubus the Teacher*, the montage *D.E.* (based on Ehrenburg's novel), and Tretyakov's *The Earth in Turmoil* – the research group arrived at what Fyodorov called 'the specific gravity' of each production. Thereafter, the relative distributions of the standard reactions in the different productions were compared. Although several statistical charts were presented, Fyodorov did not formulate any more far-reaching conclusions on the basis of the experiment than the 'rule of thumb' that in any comedy, 'laughter should make up no less than 70 per cent of the audience reactions (otherwise the performance will be boring)'.[12]

Fyodorov's article provoked an immediate response from Mikhail Zagorsky. Referring to his earlier work in the field and his article in *Lef* the year before, Zagorsky contended that the precondition for serious audience research was a more differentiated concept of the audience than that presented by the Meyerhold theatre's research team. In his view, more important than noting a greater volume of laughter in one production than in another was

investigating from *which social groups and layers* the audience was drawn, *the way in which* each group reacted, and *what* it really reacted *to* in a given performance. Who reacts *when*, *how*, and *to what* – this is what we want to know when we talk about audience surveys today.[13]

Zagorsky contended that, because the single, unified auditorium was a fiction, the registration of responses of the audience *en bloc* as made by the Meyerhold team had no information value; instead, he supported the questionnaire method.

Soon after the appearance of Zagorsky's article, Professor Aleksey Gvozdev, head of the Theatre Department of the State Institute for the History of the Arts in Leningrad and a close ally of Meyerhold, entered the debate on the side of Fyodorov and the audience research experiments he had reported on.[14] Gvozdev argued that Zagorsky was mistaken in his contention that of the questions *who*, *when*, *how*, and *to what*, only the third (*how*) had been studied at the Meyerhold theatre. To answer the questions *when* and *to what*, however, the complete scripts of the plays had to be published and, of course, this was not possible in a journal like *Life of Art*. As for the question *who*, Gvozdev denied that 'the audience' was merely a fiction. The theatre scholar had no other material at his disposal than the spontaneously gathered, 'mixed' audience. The regular audiences of the professional theatres were the only ones that could be studied *systematically* and in a long series of *repeated experiments* – two conditions that had to be met by any research method with pretensions to being scientific.

Gvozdev dismissed Zagorsky's own single experiment in 1920–1 with audience questionnaires (completed by only 186 of an unknown number of spectators actually present) as amateurish. The scientifically correct way to answer the four questions posed by Zagorsky, he said, was through a *comparison* between the general picture of audience responses already at hand and the responses of an audience whose homogeneous social background could be verified. In practice, however, the task of gathering a 'socially homogeneous audience' – for example, of 'workers from the workbench' – was not so simple. Here too, objective, empirical criteria had to be applied. The importance of the work done by the Meyerhold theatre research group, Gvozdev said, was that it had laid 'a concrete foundation for scientific audience research'. If in the future one could introduce changes into a production as an experiment, in order to test the change in audience reactions, Gvozdev concluded, then new perspectives opened up for detailed empirical studies.

Vasily Fyodorov himself replied to Zagorsky's attacks in the following issue of *Life of Art*, elaborating his criticism of the questionnaire method as totally invalid.[15] It was not the subjective impressions of the spectators themselves – jotted down spontaneously or, even worse, 'at home in the evening over tea'! – but only an objective recording of reactions in the auditorium that could lead to solid knowledge about the functioning of the performance.

In order to pinpoint the interrelationship between the reactions of the audience and the actual performance, the research team at the Meyerhold theatre also recorded a vast number of other facts every night. In addition to the responses of the audience, these included which actors were on duty (Russian theatres often work with changes in cast), a time-and-motion study ('chronometrage'[16]) including the length of pauses and intervals, the performance of the actors, the work of the stage hands, box-office receipts, and finally, comments by the director or assistants. Fyodorov therefore argued that changes in the intended reactions of the audience could be immediately traced to changes in the work of the staff, and that the latter could be corrected.[17] As for questionnaires, he could accept them only as a means of refining the objective methods applied, not as a method in itself.[18]

Before the discussion on the pages of *Life of Art* ended with a further pair of rejoinders from Zagorsky and Fyodorov, repeating their criticism of the behaviourist and questionnaire methods, respectively, a third point of view on audience research was introduced.[19] The director Alexander Bardovsky, who had used questionnaires as early as 1917,[20] reported that his theatre, the Leningrad Youth Theatre, had experimented with audience response research during the past 1924–5 season independently of the Meyerhold theatre. Bardovsky argued the usefulness of questionnaires for both directors and actors. The weakness of the method, however, was that the questionnaires recorded only the final reactions of the spectator, not those experienced *during* the actual performance. In order to register these, the Leningrad Youth Theatre had used what Bardovsky called an individual method. Instead of recording 'the common denominator' of the audience, as proposed by Fyodorov and the Meyerhold theatre, Bardovsky's assistants had scrupulously registered 'the reactions of single, outstandingly typical children' and then summed them up in a 'general survey'. This type of 'individual objective' method had in fact been introduced very early in Russian children's theatre and was used at least throughout the 1920s.[21]

The interest of the Meyerhold theatre and the Leningrad Youth Theatre was clearly practical: they were seeking methods to check the responses provoked by the stimuli emitted from the stage. By 'responses' they thought only of the *empirically measurable* reactions of the spectators in the auditorium. How the stimuli on stage were interpreted by the spectators and what the reactions of the audience in turn really meant was never asked by the research teams. In fact, no one participating in the discussion in *Life of Art* had posed the question of the *experiences* of the theatre spectator and how to find methods to describe them. In other words, no one had complemented Zagorsky's four questions – who, when, how, and to what – with the essential fifth one: *why*?

This important addition was made by Mikhail Zagorsky himself in a kind of postscript to the discussion in *Life of Art*, published in another theatre journal, *Novyi zritel* (*The New Spectator*).[22] Zagorsky criticised Professor Gvozdev's proposal of confronting the responses of 'the mixed audience' with an objectively reviewed audience of 'workers from the workbench' as an effort to correct one abstraction with the help of another.

Who laughed at a certain line in 'the mixed audience'? A Komsomol member, a bourgeois, an intellectual? – I don't know, answers Gvozdev, it was 'the audience' that laughed. And who were these 'workers from the workbench'? Proletarians brought up in the city or newly urbanised peasants who have only just begun to be recast in the big melting pot of the factory? Were they young or old, literate or illiterate? Why did they remain silent at a moment where the mixed audience laughed, and what was the meaning of this silence?

By asking *why* the spectators would respond in this way or that way, Zagorsky had undoubtedly moved the whole discussion on to a new level. His summing-up of the empiricist limitations of Gvozdev's – and, essentially, the Meyerhold theatre research team's – project was devastating:

To all these questions, Gvozdev has no answer, because they do not fit into the 'scientific method' he recommends. He operates with the fictions of 'the audience' or 'the workers from the workbench' and their outward behaviour without trying to explain the concrete nature of the given spectator and the inner meaning of his emotions.

Zagorsky had no real alternative proposals for future audience research, apart from further developing the sociological aspect of the questionnaire method. Nevertheless, his criticism of the Meyerhold theatre research project was important in two ways. First, it marked the downfall of the myth of the audience as a homogeneous entity, representative of the collective as a whole. Each of the participants in the *Life of Art* discussion agreed that the audience had to be studied closely, that is, that its character could no longer be regarded as self-evident; the days when the spectator could be called 'a model of Soviet Russia' without anyone protesting seemed to be long past. Secondly, Zagorsky's opposition to the 'objective' methods of Meyerhold's research assistants had led him to a critique of the behaviourist approach to aesthetics which was perhaps more far-reaching than he himself realised.

Two concepts of the audience

The extensive 1925 discussion of the spectator had provided at least a hint of new perspectives on the theatre as a form of communication. The great myth of the representative auditorium, which had been a fundamental element in the ideology of theatrical reformers and revolutionaries for more than half a century, had quite obviously begun to fall apart. Two possible strategies for further development were already becoming clearly visible. One consisted of an endless series of attempts to maintain the idea of the 'total' theatre by means of arguments borrowed from biology, depth psychology, religion or other disciplines mobilised for the purpose. The other was an at once much more modest and more realistic view of the theatre according to which the spectator would no longer be regarded as an object to be acted upon by the artist but as a conscious and productive subject.

The first approach had in effect been developed as early as the beginning of the 1920s by Meyerhold's 'rational' theatre, in which the rationality was entirely reserved to the director and the actors and the role of the audience was by contrast seen as wholly ideologised and defined as the experience of and reaction to the conditions set by the director.[23]

The notion of the ritual theatre in its purest form was, by 1925, dead and buried. It had never really appealed to Meyerhold, for whom the original Wagnerian utopia – the great spectacle performed for the 'representative' auditorium – was quite adequate as an ideological foundation. The total hold the director maintained by all available means on the audience now seemed in itself to have replaced the social and moral community that Wagner had at least posited as a desirable goal. With the reservation that Meyerhold was probably always more a Wagnerian than a Marxist, we can agree with Helen Krich Chinoy's observation that the phenomenon was not unique either to him or to the Soviet Union:

> The personal distillation of the director was the modern substitute for the whole complex of social and theatrical factors that had once made theatre the great collective art. Reinhardt illustrates this process in its baroque, Wagnerian aspect. Vsevolod Meyerhold illustrates it in its constructivist, Marxian aspect.[24]

The other approach that was hinted at in the 1925 discussion leads sharply away from the dream of making the theatre socially useful by bringing it back to ritual or some other 'collective wellspring'. Although this second line also views the spectators as the 'basic material' of the theatre, they are no longer an object (as in the 'theatre of attractions') but a subject. Even today, sixty years later, it would be wrong to say that this approach has triumphed or displaced the post-Wagnerian view, but the Soviet debate can be regarded as symptomatic of an approaching up-

heaval. Precisely as a symptom, for the discussion undoubtedly beto-
kened an upheaval or at least a crisis in the practical work of the theatre.
It was hardly a coincidence that the crisis became as acute and as quickly
apparent as it did in the Russian theatre, in which the question of the
relationship between stage and auditorium had been so emphatically
posed.

Chapter 10

The Theatre as an Arena for Discussion

The divided audience

The crisis in the political 'total' theatre was a fact that could not be avoided by even the most elaborate devices for controlling audience reactions. The notions of the homogeneous audience and the uniform impact of the performance had been shown to be untenable. The external causes of this were obviously the rapidly growing social and cultural conflicts of NEP reality, but we have seen that the intrinsic development of the Russian theatre had also questioned those notions on the level of aesthetic theory.

In the spring of 1926, Sergey Tretyakov presented to Meyerhold a new play, *I Want a Child*, in which he set out to approach the relationship between stage and auditorium from a new angle. The spectators would still gather together in order to be subjected – and perhaps again as representatives of the collective – to powerful effects from the stage. The point of departure, however, was no longer the postulated *unity* of the auditorium that was to be manifested and confirmed by the performance, but instead the socially based and by now undeniable *division* in the audience.

Biology and society

In contrast to Tretyakov's preceding plays, *I Want a Child* was based not
on documentary fact but on a kind of hypothesis, a conflict between an
individual brimming with utopian radicalism and a reality that was
proving difficult to change. The protagonist is Milda, a young Communist and cultural worker who organises the women in a communal
apartment building. The time is 'today', that is, about 1925.

Milda's political commitment is to the collective, especially the women
and young people, but her motivation is exclusively rational:

> There is no such thing as human solidarity. There are only well-
> equipped factories. A correctly planned day. A network of militia
> stations. A precise railroad timetable and a correctly plotted course
> toward socialism.[1]

Her sexual instincts, which in the play are depicted as entirely directed
toward reproduction and motherhood, Milda also attempts to guide into
rational channels. She intensely desires a child, but it is not to be
begotten randomly and unconsciously. She finds a strong young worker,
Yakov, to impregnate her, but when he wants to continue the relationship she rebuffs him, citing their agreement that they go on seeing each
other only until the pregnancy is certain.

Set against Milda is the entire chaotic reality of NEP: a society
plagued by shortages and rapidly growing class differences that make
the achievements of the October Revolution and the political slogans of
yesterday appear anything but credible. Hooligans rape young girls on
the street. Prostitution, alcoholism and venereal disease are a part of
everyday life. In the partitioned 'communalised' apartments people live
like caged animals.

Probably not even Mayakovsky's *The Bedbug* painted such a glaring
picture of life under NEP.[2] Today, Tretyakov's play reads almost as a
satirical allegory on Gorbachev's post-perestroika Russia: under the
fading red banners of the past – hustling, the shady dealings of racketeers
and the Party, the desperate efforts of ordinary people to cope with
inflation and shortages.

However, *I Want a Child* is not a naturalistic drama in which the
environment assumes the rôle of Fate. The play is a rapidly developing
melodrama with hilarious farcical scenes where situations of coincidence and misunderstanding serve to unmask the 'false' self-consciousness of the characters surrounding Milda. There is not a single scene,
however, that seems to change the image of the heroine. Milda is

straightforward, she has no tragic choices to make, and least of all is there any growing self-understanding on her part. In the final scene, action is abruptly projected into the future of 1930. An ideal new day-care centre has been built, and in a carnivalesque 'baby fair', Milda and Yakov's wife (ex-rivals) share the first prize for the healthiest child in the nursery.

The young heroine is in all respects an exception in the workers' collective. She is not Russian but Latvian, the trousers and tie she wears are programmatically 'unwomanly', and she is the sole representative of the young Communist intelligentsia. She is categorical in her demands on herself and extreme in her rationalism. She is an uncommon, not to say superhuman, individual; it is no coincidence that she bears the name of the ancient Baltic goddess of love (Tretyakov spoke Latvian), although her love has been entirely transformed into rationality and utility. Everything about Milda – her maximalism, her resentment of ordinary human frailty, her idea of motherhood – can be construed as so many fanatical projections of her disappointment with Soviet reality. Milda wants *the future now*, and the more disappointing the actual results of the revolution, the more she wants to give birth to a baby, that is, the Man of the Future. In this respect she is a pathetic character, although her insensitivity to typically human feelings (love, jealousy, fear) is also shown with comical distance.[3]

I Want a Child, with its 'daring' theme and its satirical exposé of NEP reality, could not be approved by the Soviet censors of 1926 even for an experimental theatre such as Meyerhold's. Discussions of a revision were begun and resumed several times. In late September 1926 Tretyakov concluded a contract, but soon it was announced that after a reading of the text the Meyerhold theatre had decided that the author should rework it. In January 1927 Tretyakov delivered a new version and rehearsals started.

The revision was so comprehensive that we can agree with Fritz Mierau, who speaks of two different plays.[4] The most significant difference consists of radical cuts in the scenes depicting the squalor and brutality of life in the working-class district. The social theme was thus critically reduced, and Milda's search for a biologically superior father for her child and the triangular conflict between her, Yakov, and his sweetheart became correspondingly more prominent. The biological or eugenic element was further accentuated by the fact that Milda was no longer primarily a political organiser but an agronomist who, in a newly written opening scene, visits a kolkhoz and discusses scientific methods of animal husbandry.

Quantitatively, the revision shortened the text by about a third. Qualitatively, it transformed *I Want a Child* from an explosive political play about the conflict between frustrated utopianism and social destitution under NEP into a discussion of eugenics as such in socialist society. Criticism of NEP from a sociological point of view was surely much more difficult to pursue in the Soviet Union of 1927 than a discussion of 'rational eugenics', which in the 1920s was a common topic both there and in liberal and socialist circles in the West.[5] Censorship problems, however, were probably not the main reason for the shift of emphasis. In abandoning the political satire on NEP – which other playwrights were exploiting with great success – Tretyakov sought to stage a confrontation between old and new and revive, at least on a thematic level, the constructivist concept of theatre as 'the factory for the new man'.

Meyerhold rehearsed the play sporadically during the 1927–8 season, but the theatre had still not been granted permission to stage it. At two meetings at the censorship offices in December 1928, Meyerhold and the young Leningrad director Igor Terentev, who was known for his penchant for shocking effects, were invited to present their rival plans for a production of *I Want a Child*. Both projects included experiments with audience participation in the performance. Terentev wanted to use an extensive technical apparatus: by means of closed-circuit radio, during the play the audience would be able to consult a staff of experts in a glass cubicle above their heads. Meyerhold swiftly appropriated his younger colleague's idea and went a step farther. He proposed that questions from the audience to the actors and experts in the auditorium should interrupt the action, arguing that this was demanded by the 'difficult' subject of the play. At the same time, Meyerhold said, this 'play-discussion' would provide an opportunity to revive the improvisational techniques of his beloved *commedia dell'arte*. For all the differences in their projects, both Terentev and Meyerhold viewed the inclusion of audience responses into the actual performance as a means of extending the director's hold on the audience in a 'total' theatrical event.[6]

The censors finally awarded Meyerhold's theatre exclusive staging rights to *I Want a Child*. Rehearsals were resumed in January 1929. The constructivist designer El Lissitsky, who had already been invited to do the set, quickly came up with a complete model. For various reasons, however, work was soon halted again, this time indefinitely.[7] Still, the available sources permit us to make some observations on the planned production.

Together with Meyerhold, Lissitsky intended to stage Tretyakov's play in an amphitheatre that would physically unite actors and spectators under the control of the director, a form that only the symbolist utopians had earlier proposed in Russia. The acting space was to be elliptic, surrounded by the audience: the balcony would be dressed in slogans such as 'A HEALTHY CHILD IS THE FUTURE OF SOCIALISM'. The stage design, as often in Meyerhold's theatre, was to be multi-levelled: bridges would connect the acting space with the balcony, and the stage floor would be transparent, permitting lighting effects and projections from below. Everything inside the elliptic space would thus be ruled by the principles of openness, simultaneity and transparency. This was in accordance with Meyerhold's interpretation of Tretyakov's play as an open structure with no cathartic resolution. The physically joined audience and stage, however, were not to unite in ritual enthusiasm; on the contrary, the 'psychological footlights', as in Meyerhold's theatre before the revolution, would instead be stressed by the spatial arrangements (cf. above p. 52). Under bright floodlights the discord both between stage and audience and within the audience was to be revealed, and open discussion was to be provoked on the themes of sex, procreation and the New Man.

This was, so to speak, the programmatic, rational aspect of the ambitious joint enterprise of three leading representatives of early 1920s constructivism. If we go beyond the declarations briefly and take a second look at the whole project, however, we will discover a profound symbolism with surprisingly archaic connotations.

The elliptic form of Lissitsky's amphitheatre is an *oval*. It can, in fact, be interpreted as an egg or a womb: the space in which the New Man is to be conceived. Milda's idea is to procreate this New Man basically all by herself – through her own rational calculations, through the supremacy of her mind over matter. In a sense she is herself an avant-garde creator in everyday life. But her dream of producing a child without a father, without love, under controlled circumstances, is at the same time a modern version of the ancient Homunculus project. This aspect is strongly supported by Lissitsky's laboratory-like set of glass and steel constructions. However, even more can be said of the spatial symbolism of the planned production. In the discussions with the censors, Meyerhold said that the characters in the play should be shown in the manner of 'students dissecting corpses in an anatomical theatre', a metaphor which Tretyakov soon paraphrased as 'love laid upon the operating table'. This feature can also be traced in Lissitsky's project. The clinically bright light of the amphitheatre recalls the anatomical theatre of the seventeenth century, in which the universal scientist, as in the concoction of the Homunculus, set himself on an equal footing with God when he peered into the human body that theretofore had been the secret of the First Creator alone.

The symbolism of the constructivist amphitheatre for *I Want a Child*, which at first glance might seem remote from the pronounced rationalism of the whole enterprise, is thus complex but consistent. 'Bourgeois' love is to be laid out before the eyes of the spectators upon the vivisection table in the elliptic space. At the same time, a process of creation is taking place: the New Man is being produced in the laboratory conditions of the theatre. The masters of art thus unite with science and once again propose the utopian 'transformation of everyday life'.

'Love on the operating table'

During the discussions in the censorship offices, Tretyakov did not seem enthusiastic about Meyerhold's proposal. Once the decision was taken in favour of it, however, he immediately embraced the idea of combining the play and discussion and wrote an article which even radicalised it. The audience should not perceive the play in a 'sexual-aesthetic' mode, Tretyakov stressed, but should view it 'rather as one regards an anatomical atlas'. He went on to outline an aesthetics that pointed out of the theatre toward actual social practice:

> I am no believer in plays whose dramaturgical climax is some sort of generally accepted maxim that restores the equilibrium between the forces struggling on stage. When the plot has been resolved and the moral delivered the spectators can calmly go out and put on their galoshes.
>
> I find greater value in plays that reach their conclusion out among the spectators beyond the walls of the auditorium.
>
> Not a play that ends by closing an aesthetic circle, but a play that takes a running jump from the aesthetic trampoline of the stage and then continues in a spiral whose loops are consistent in the discussions and extra-theatrical practice of the spectators.
>
> Love on stage has thus far been a provocative spice. It has kept the spectators tense and transformed them into 'vicarious lovers'.
>
> In *I Want a Child* love has been laid upon the operating table and studied with respect to its social consequences.[8]

I have quoted this passage at some length because it contains a summary yet very clearly formulated notion of the theatre that deviates radically from both the naturalistic aesthetics of empathy and the concept of 'processing the spectator' that Tretyakov himself had earlier so passionately advocated. Proceeding from the view that NEP had accelerated the division of society and that the previous, unifying conceptions of the theatre were now inadequate, Tretyakov proposed a theatre that regards the spectator as neither a sentient subject (as in Naturalism) nor a controlled object (as in the theatre of attractions) but as a rational, active subject. Certainly the presupposition was that rational spectators, when they are free, will reach only ideologically 'correct' conclusions.

One must of course beware of ascribing to Tretyakov a full-blown theory, let alone practice, on the basis of one short article. Nevertheless, the theses he proposes seem to indicate that he was drawing more extensive conclusions than his directors expected from the recent discussion on the audience. He recognises that both the unity of the audience and that between auditorium and stage have gone. Furthermore, he does not call on the 'total' director to restore it and thus provide a social legitimisation of art. The social function of theatre must instead be given a different foundation: the extra-theatrical, rational rather than emotional responses of a heterogeneous, 'non-representative' auditorium. This notion, as well as certain striking formulations in Tretyakov's 1929 article, inevitably recalls another contemporary dramatist who was likewise interested in a theatre that operated on the basis of contradiction rather than unity, namely Bertolt Brecht.

Brecht, Tretyakov and the instructive theatre

Erwin Piscator had developed a political theatre in Berlin in the 1920s that in many respects was not only analogous with but directly influenced by the experiments of Meyerhold and the constructivists. All means at the disposal of the modern theatrical machine were brought into play to achieve optimal agitational effect. Piscator himself describes as follows the reception of one of his famous productions, the 'mammoth historical revue' *Trotz alledem!* which dealt with the revolutionary workers' movement in 1914–19 and was staged during the German Communist Party Convention in 1925:

> The people who filled the house had for the most part been actively involved in the period, and what we were showing them was in a true sense their own fate, their own tragedy being acted out before their eyes. Theatre had become reality, and soon it was not a case of the

stage confronting the audience, but one big assembly, one big battle-field, one massive demonstration. It was this unity that proved that evening that political theatre could be effective agitation.[9]

The feeling that stage and auditorium had fused and that this auditorium was representative of the entire struggling working class was to Piscator proof that the theatre was necessary. We can easily recognise the Wag-nerian utopia of the great, unifying spectacle.

It was on this very issue that Bertolt Brecht would break with Piscator after several years of fruitful cooperation. Brecht would always defend the value of the technical advances made by the political *Totaltheatre*, but on the basic question of the function of the audience and the relation-ship between stage and auditorium he had parted ways with Piscator by the end of the 1920s.

What I have called 'the myth of the representative auditorium' and 'the Wagnerian utopia' were crucial elements in what Brecht referred to as 'Aristotelian' aesthetics. By this he meant not so much the classical Greek tragedy as the Wagnerian interpretation of it projected into the future which had been so influential on many theatrical reformers. It is no coincidence that one of Brecht's earliest and most famous formula-tions of the difference between the 'Aristotelian' and the new, 'epic' theatre was made on Wagner's home ground, in the (anti)opera *Mahagonny* and the notes to it (1930).[10]

In the notes to his *The Mother* (1932), Brecht described the 'Aristo-telian' view of the audience as follows:

> In calling for a direct impact, the aesthetics of the day call for an impact that flattens out all social and other distinctions between individuals. Plays of the Aristotelian type still manage to flatten out class conflicts in this way although the individuals themselves are becoming increasingly aware of class differences. The same result is achieved even when class conflicts are the subject of such plays, and even in cases where they take sides for a particular class.[11]

As long as it clings to the notion of the theatre's unifying and affirma-tive function, even the political theatre committed to 'a particular class' runs the risk of veiling rather than explaining or changing reality. At Piscator's theatre, Brecht declared in another context, this was precisely what had happened:

> The more we induced the audience to identify its own experiences

and feelings with the production, the less it learned; and the more there was to learn, the less the artistic enjoyment.[12]

Brecht's new theatrical aesthetics, especially as developed in his *Lehrstücke* from around 1930, was based on a view of the audience that departed radically from the Wagnerian or Aristotelian collective: 'Non-Aristotelian drama of *Die Mutter*'s sort is not interested in the establishment of such an entity. It divides its audience.'[13] The aim of Brecht's attempt to 'refunctionalise' the theatre was thus to combine 'aesthetic pleasure' or 'entertainment' with 'teaching', elements that in Piscator's political theatre had invariably come into conflict with each other. 'The theatre of the scientific age' aspired, so to speak, to a fusion of science and art.

Brecht often cited the *sporting event* and the *scientific demonstration* as models toward which the new, non-Aristotelian theatre should orientate itself. Diametrically opposed to the ritual, which operates solely or primarily with the signifying or symbolic function, these are dominated by the presence of the observing spectator. We should emphasise *orientate* itself toward, since the intention was not to abolish the sign function but to activate the spectator's presence and by so doing further distance the theatre from the ritual. The divorce of the theatre from ritual lamented by Wagnerians and Nietzscheans of different political persuasions was to Brecht determined by the evolution of society and needed to be neither regretted nor extolled but was quite simply a development that could and should be *used*.

> In the planetarium and the sporting arena man assumes that calmly reflective, observant and controlling attitude that has led our technicians and scientists to their discoveries. It was in the theatre, however, that human lives and attitudes should arouse interest. Modern spectators, it was thought, do not want to be passively subjected to any form of suggestion and go out of their senses by being carried away in all sorts of affective states. They do not wish to be incapacitated but want quite simply to be presented with material *that they can organise themselves*.[14]

Brecht wrote this in 1931 on his experiments of the immediately preceding years. If he had been able to read Tretyakov's explanation of the principles underlying *I Want a Child* in 1929, he would probably have rushed to get hold of the play. He did become acquainted with it some time later, at any rate, and in 1930 a German translation for the

stage was distributed: *Ich will ein Kind haben (Die Pionierin)* bearing
the note 'adapted by Bertolt Brecht'. It was also announced that a staging
was to be expected. Actually, Brecht's rôle as adapter seems for the most
part to have been limited to signing his name on the title-page; apart
from a couple of added or deleted lines that do not affect the structure of
the play, the text is a translation of the second version.[15]

It was thus this second version, in which criticism of NEP had
receded into the background and the theme of eugenics had achieved
added prominence, that was Brecht's first contact with Tretyakov's
work. The fact that the conflict between 'biological' and 'social' tended
in the play to be reduced to a conflict between 'rational' and 'spontaneous' biologism did not diminish the interest a Soviet play on the subject
probably held for Brecht.[16]

We will here refrain from discussing the relations and influences
between Tretyakov and Brecht and the exciting connection between
Soviet 'left' art and similar currents in Weimar.[17] Instead, we will limit
ourselves to summarising the parallels between the two future friends
and correspondents *before* their paths actually crossed, which, as we
know, did not happen until early 1931.

Tretyakov's 1929 article and Brecht's articles and notes in 1929–30
contain a similar critique of the contemporary theatre's view of its
audience. This criticism was levelled not least at the stages where the
two writers had themselves filled important positions (the Meyerhold
and Proletkult theatres and the *Piscator-Bühne*, respectively). Dissatis-
fied with a theatre that overpowers the spectators and renders them a
'material', both Brecht and Tretyakov were arguing for a method which
would impose on the spectator a more active, rational, and almost
scientific mode of observation.

To the earlier typology of relationships between stage and auditorium
we can now add the model of the instructive or 'epic' theatre, which has
the following distinctive features:

(1) The footlights are *marked*. The element of viewing and critical
    observation is strongly activated. No more than in the 'stylised
    theatre' are the spectators to be carried away or forced to forget
    where they are.

(2) The worlds of stage and auditorium are *incongruent*. Tretyakov's
    I Want a Child is not 'true to life' but confronts reality with a
    hypothesis, subjects a model situation to scrutiny. In Brecht's
    epic theatre the spectator is supposed to perceive something
    more than the characters themselves are able to see.

(3) The instructive or epic theatre is directed *outwards*, away from

the world of the stage. The conclusions of the instruction are to be drawn in the auditorium and specifically in real life outside the walls of the theatre.

In the light of our analysis of the 'myth of the representative auditorium' and Tretyakov's and Brecht's proposals to break with the 'Wagnerian' or 'Aristotelian' tradition, however, the typological scheme must be complemented with one more feature. The types presented above – naturalism, stylised theatre, ritual theatre and constructivism – shared a view of the auditorium as an entity directly representative of the social collective as a whole. The experience of the Proletkult Theatre, the Soviet debate on the spectator, and the practice of Piscator's political theatre in Berlin suggested that that conception was a delusion that should now be discarded. It had presumably never been anything but an ideological argument for the total theatre that promised, if only for a few hours, to heal the split inherent in class society.

Thus we can add the following feature:

(4) Unlike the other types described, the instructive or epic theatre assumes that *the audience is not homogeneous*, and in fact counteracts the establishment of emotional unity in the auditorium (this is indicated in the drawing below by a cross). In contrast to the earlier types, the instructive theatre does not propose to achieve in the theatre what is impossible in society. The theatre is only a model of reality, but this 'only' is at the same time its strength. Social conflicts must be resolved in society, not in the theatre, but the model can suggest new approaches to their resolution.

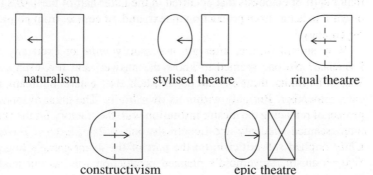

naturalism   stylised theatre   ritual theatre

constructivism   epic theatre

Chapter 11

The Provisional Abdication of Total Theatre

The halted production of Tretyakov's *I Want a Child* marked the end of a period of intense experimentation with forms thought rational for influencing the audience as a whole. The idea of the total theatre with its myth of the representative auditorium had lost its attraction in Soviet Russia, at least for the time being, and at least in its politicised version. The age was post-revolutionary and pre-Stalinist at the same time. General issues could no longer be approached outside the framework of the taboos and musts of the current political line without incurring the intervention of the censors, but in private matters pluralism was flourishing. This situation is consistent with and may even partly explain the major shift of emphasis that occurred in the latter half of the 1920s from director to actor, from production to text, and, of course, from politics to psychology.[1]

Why should theatre, after all, necessarily *unite* or exert any total influence? No one seemed to know the answer, and few even cared. Within its limits, theatre could do so much else: entertain, dream, educate, remember. But only within its own limits. The great avant-garde project of replacing the theatre institution with the 'factory for the skilled man' seemed suddenly and hopelessly out of date. Even if *I Want a Child* implied self-criticism on the part of the avant-garde's lingering Wagnerianism, Meyerhold's planned production was, as our analysis has intimated, basically an extension of the same tradition.

In an article written in the autumn of 1927 (after the second version of *I Want a Child*) Sergey Tretyakov presented a series of pertinent but also unusually melancholic reflections on the current state of Soviet dramaturgy. Summarising, he noted that the results of the 'October Revolution of the Theatre' were nil:

> The confrontation of 'life' and 'art' is over. What is left are confrontations between different styles within 'art'. Theatre has returned to its channels, constructions have become decent wooden sets, and biomechanics a peculiar kind of plastic movement.

For a man who had been involved in some of the most radical theatrical experiments of his time, this statement is self-critical indeed. As for the current situation, Tretyakov was equally pessimistic. Playwrights who attempt to address a burning contemporary topic on the stage discover that the issue is first of all deformed by the conventional forms of the theatre, and secondly, that it has usually lost its topicality by the time the production finally reaches opening night.

According to Tretyakov, the playwright who still insisted that the theatre perform an activating function had but two alternatives:

> either to learn to foresee future, as yet unarticulated questions, or to turn to the club stage on the ground level, which can deal with truly local themes in the shortest possible time.[2]

The 'futuristic' alternative had been attempted by Tretyakov in *I Want a Child*. The 'ground level' alternative to being absorbed into the theatre institution – which according to Tretyakov was irrespective of 'style' bound to emasculate any non-aesthetic matter – still had to be tested in practice. But we know what the writer had in mind. It was the new movement of small political theatre groups – the 'guerrilla theatres' of that time.

As early as 1924, when the crisis in the avant-garde theatre was just beginning to make itself felt, Osip Brik had declared that it was not in the theatres but in the workers' clubs that the important theatrical innovations were now to be found.[13] Brik was referring to the workers' club theatre movement, the best-known representatives of which became the Blue Blouse groups that blossomed in the mid-1920s and soon had offshoots all over Europe. Developing from the amateur theatre movement, the Blue Blouses adopted many of the innovations of Meyerhold and his followers (such as striking juxtapositions of text and physical movement) but took exception to the avant-garde's grand theories with

Osip Brik
'Not in the Theatre but in the Club!'

The theatre thrashes around in its little box and cannot get out.

No help is to be had here from masters of ceremonies, strolls out among the audience, performances 'out in the provinces', topical interpolations in the text or other such sallies on the part of the actor, walled in as he is by the footlights.

Attempts have been made to explode the theatre 'from within'. In vain. The expert dynamiters conscientiously expended their supplies of dynamite – but the result was unexpected:

Instead of an explosion, a brilliant pyrotechnical display glorifying that same bastion of theatricality (cf. Meyerhold's 'The Forest', Tairov's 'The Storm', etc.).

But must the theatre be blown up? Let it stand as a monument to art and olden times.

The new theatricality is taking shape without it and outside it – not in special little theatre boxes, but in the midst of the spectators – *in the clubs*!

Of course, not on the old club stages straining to imitate the 'real' theatres, but in our new clubs that are free of academic traditions.

Here *there are no plays* – there are only *scenarios*.

Not topical *interpolations*, but a thoroughly topical *text*.

Not 'contact' between actor and people, but a blood relationship.

Not the pinning-up of agitational pennants, but a single agitational task.

Not causuistic motivation of why Ostrovsky is useful to the people, but clear utilitarianism.

Not props, but reality.

Not the amusing fireworks of the unfortunate dynamiters, but the living fire of modern theatricality.

The new club has allies in the theatrical world: the *circus* and the *variety stage*.

They have what it needs.

It is through their water of life that the old theatre man will rediscover his youth.

But remember the fairy tale?

'The tsar jumped into the pot and was cooked.
But Ivanushka the fool came out of the pot handsome and wise.'

From *Lef*, No. 1 (5) (1924)

---

regard to the audience. In the terminology of production aesthetics, they stayed strictly within the limits of the 'minimum programme' of political agitation and satire. For all their hilarious 'post-eccentrism', however, the Blue Blouses were not only strictly pragmatic but also under obvious political control. It hardly occurred to them to stage a provocative sketch on a 'difficult', that is, not officially sanctioned political, social, or ethical theme.[4]

Osip Brik's contention in 1924 that the new theatricalism was the exclusive creation of the little workers' troupes, of course, was deliberately provocative. In a slightly longer perspective it was simply wrong. Suffice it to mention a few of the achievements of the Russian theatre in the years 1925–30: Meyerhold's production of *The Government Inspector*; Kamerny Theatre's productions of O'Neill; the 'rejuvenated' Stanislavsky's *Le Mariage de Figaro*; or Igor Terentev's sensational *Government Inspector* in the little Leningrad Journalists' Club Theatre. In all these historic productions and in many others, theatricalism was paramount. All expressive stage devices, all possible variations of the interrelationship between stage and audience, were used on the highest level of artistic consciousness. In a sense, the late 1920s were the time of harvest for Russian theatrical modernism as a historical formation.[5]

From one point of view, however, Osip Brik turns out to have been right – as was often the case, more correct in his analysis than in his prognosis. The workers' club stages certainly did not accomplish any shift, either artistically or politically, in the evolution of the theatre. Still, the professional theatre of the latter half of the 1920s was not quite what it used to be. It was a theatre that had abdicated its former great social ambitions. For the moment, at least, disenchantment with the myth of the representative audience was overwhelming. Almost everyone seemed to agree in practice with Alexander Tairov's well-known dictum: 'Theatre is theatre'.[6]

The exception to the rule, of course, was Meyerhold – always in the centre of events, always against the stream. It was through his theatre, although not by him personally, that the extensive 1925 discussion on the nature of the theatrical audience and its modes of reception was initiated. The Master himself was at this time totally absorbed by what was to become one of his greatest productions ever, *The Government Inspector* (which opened on 9 December 1926). This transformation of Gogol's comedy into a sombre social tragedy, an investigation of the besetting Russian sins, was at the same time Meyerhold's contribution to the critique of 'total' theatre, and his reconfirmation of that theatre. His *Government Inspector* recalled in several ways the whole society's self-interrogation in Greek tragedy.[7] The spectators were confronted with a multi-faceted theatrical magic mirror (very different from the naturalist 'reflection of life') which probed both their conscious and subconscious, understood as belonging to a collective consciousness. The multi-perspective, cinematic composition of the performance created a complex structure which allowed for each spectator an individual perception of the action, yet captured each individual in a shared suggestive atmosphere of tragi-farce in slow motion. In the opinion of many critics and spectators, Meyerhold's reinterpretation of Gogol managed to recreate dialectically the unified character of the auditorium of the ancient tragedy. The intention, however, was not to demonstrate any utopian or utilitarian notions, as in the constructivist productions, but rather to provoke everyone gathered in the theatre to question themselves.

Was the myth of the representative auditorium, then, not *only* a myth after all? Meyerhold's further investigations into the self-consciousness of Russian and Soviet society (begun early in his career and continued in the 1920s through productions of Griboyedov, Erdman, Mayakovsky, Pushkin) oblige us – in his case, at least – to leave the question open. Perhaps it is enough to say that for Meyerhold the myth – sometimes – actually *did* work.

Soon the Stalinist policy of 'national' unanimity and obligatory optimism was to confront the Soviet Russian theatre with tasks quite different from tragi-comic self-reflection. To the forgers of the new monolithic ideology, the familiar notions of the representative auditorium and of theatre which confirm the unity of the masses seemed to be convenient vehicles for the organisation of ideological coalescence. Thus once again myth was to be declared reality. Certain notions from the debates analysed above were soon to return in the form of a grim parody, under the banner of Socialist Realism – as if the controversies had never taken place and the questions they leave us with had never been raised.

In fact, of course, nothing was forgotten, but a very great deal was repressed and censored – officially, implicitly, and in private. The post-October discourse on art and its social significance had made its inevitable imprint both on the minds of the participants and on the memory of the seemingly passive observers. As the 1930s approached, an entire arsenal of arguments, counter-arguments, and rhetorical structures were prepared which eventually would be reactivated, sometimes in new guises, and sometimes even turned against their original authors.[8]

Postscript:
the Avant-Garde and History

For the suppressed history of the Russian avant-garde, the 1970s were the great years of rehabilitation. They witnessed the publication of numerous pioneering studies based on archival research, the reprinting and translation of anthologies of manifestos, and the arrangement of retrospective exhibitions. The process culminated in the giant 1979 exhibition 'Paris–Moscou' at the Centre Georges Pompidou in Paris.[1]

The magnificent revival of the Russian avant-garde heritage through the efforts of devoted researchers and museum curators, however, contained a paradox: in a sense, it perpetuated the historiography it set out to replace. The official Soviet art history of the period tended at best to describe the first turbulent years under Bolshevik rule in a teleological perspective as a transitional interval leading toward the ultimate goal of establishing Socialist Realism. The Western rehabilitationist version generally adhered to the same evolutionary scheme, except that the transition was evaluated negatively as a period of growing restrictions and Party control which ultimately sought to suppress abstract art, futurism, formalist criticism, and so on. In this perspective, the physical annihilation of many avant-gardists during the purges merely served to confirm their image as victims and martyrs of the Stalinist conspiracy against free creativity.

The picture of the Soviet 1920s as a utopia of cultural experiment that was methodically strangled by the cold hand of the Party, however, has undergone a radical revision in the past decade. Solzhenitsyn's GULAG has become an everyday cliché, although those who use it are not always aware that the writer dates the construction of the first camps to the time of Lenin. Professional historians have devoted enormous attention to the question of the roots of the Stalinist political and cultural system. In the

West, anti-utopian reflection has become an important component of the general reassessment of the 'modernist project'. In this context, the earlier dualistic – and basically moralistic – conception of the Soviet Russian avant-garde as merely a victim of the Stalinist dictatorship has necessarily yielded to more dialectical and detached analysis. One interesting example of this change is a book by Boris Groys provocatively entitled *Gesamtkunstwerk Stalin* (1988).

The vital task which Groys (a Russian philosopher and art critic living in Germany) undertakes in his book is to dissolve the earlier black-and-white conceptions. Noting that Socialist Realism is usually interpreted as the absolute antithesis of the formalist avant-garde, Groys proposes instead to 'focus on its continuity with the avant-garde project, even though the realisation of that project differed from the avant-garde vision'.[2] Basing his approach both on recent research in the history of Russian art and on post-modernist theory, Groys attempts to define not what *separates* the avant-garde and Stalinist culture, but what *connects* them. This, he maintains, has become possible in the light of recent 'post-utopian' tendencies in Russian art (often summarised as '*sots-art*', a combination of 'Socialist Realism' and 'pop art'), whose dissolution of totalitarian clichés in an ironic play of quotation and duplication also 'lays bare' certain classical avant-garde postulates. I shall limit myself here to discussing the thesis that the avant-garde shared in the invention of the great 'synthetic work of art' of Stalinist culture.

According to Groys, the basic topos of the avant-garde was the shift from 'representing to transforming the world'.[3] This notion is familiar to us from the analysis above, as is its corollary: when art had thus lost its secondary, autonomous character in relation to reality, this reality itself became material whose immanent resistance the avant-garde artist was to overcome. As a matter of fact, Groys says, the avant-garde was permeated by a 'will to power' which after the October Revolution expanded into the realm of cultural and even political power, where it finally clashed with that of the Bolsheviks. The myth of the 'innocence' of the avant-garde cannot be sustained, Groys stresses. The sombre fate of many avant-garde artists was not that of martyrs: they ended up isolated both from the power they coveted and from the opposition ('fellow travellers' or 'inner émigrés') they scorned, and defenceless against ideological attacks of the sort they themselves had 'rehearsed' in 1918 or 1919.[4]

The brutal politicisation of the cultural discourse, however, was only a minor contribution of the avant-garde to the Socialist Realist edifice. The kernel of its 'will to power' was the claim to possess transcendent

knowledge about the essence of reality, and consequently the right to
control reality. On the surface, the avant-garde was rational and utilitarian – the absolute opposite, it would seem, of the ideological dream
factory of Socialist Realism. As we have shown in the analysis of the
theatrical avant-garde, however, this rationality remained the privilege
of the artist/director – the 'moulder of life' – and it was in addition of a
peculiar kind. The material of art was understood in a far from material-
ist way, which Groys traces directly to the Russian tradition of 'objective' symbolist aesthetics. In the final analysis, the language of 'pure'
forms, 'pure' movement, and so on, reveals itself to be the vehicle of an
objective, Neo-Platonic essence constituting the basis for the attempted
avant-gardist intervention in reality which culminated in the construction of the New Man.[5]

It is in this 'demiurgic' aspect of the avant-garde, often overshadowed
by utilitarian and rationalist slogans, that Boris Groys perceives the
connection with Socialist Realism and the *Gesamtkunstwerk* of Stalinist
culture. Both in Soviet criticism and in Western 'rehabilitationism',
Socialist Realism is usually viewed as the total negation of the avant-
garde. Groys objects that it was in fact not the *rejection* but the
radicalisation of the avant-garde project: 'Socialist Realism can be said
to be the continuation of the Russian avant-garde's strategy by other
means'.[6]

The question of these *means*, however, is a crucial one. The avant-
garde was part of the tradition it opposed, even if it saw itself as the end
of art history, and it always insisted on the connection between artistic
technique and ideology. The debate on the monuments is exemplary: the
'dead forms' of representational art were considered inadmissable in the
projected new society. (This is a point on which today's post-modernist
art of quotation, ironical duplication, and 'simulacrum' radically differs
from the classical avant-garde.)

For all its eulogies on the 'progressive' heritage of the past, Groys
maintains, Socialist Realism was much more radical than the avant-
garde in its break with the European artistic tradition. It would be a
mistake to view Socialist Realism as simply a regression to a situation
before the avant-garde; it is instead a 'negation of the negation'. Thus
Stalinist culture is beyond style: radically eclectic, radically ahistorical,
radically arbitrary. (This 'post-modernist' aspect of Stalinist culture is
easily observable in architecture.)

This ambition to implement the avant-garde utopian project by non-
avant-garde, traditionalist, 'realistic' means constitutes the very es-

sence of this culture and therefore cannot be dismissed as a superficial pose. The life-building spirit of the Stalin years resists interpretation as a mere regression into the past, because it insists that it is an absolute apocalyptic future in which distinguishing between past and future is no longer meaningful.[7]

Boris Groys' interpretation of the evolution of Russian art in the twentieth century is radical but also methodologically consistent. Groys 'reads' the avant-garde project and Socialist Realism as two great myths, the first consistently subsumed into the second. From the point of view of analysis, the fact that one myth produced artistic masterpieces and the other kitsch and violence is of no concern to the author. There is, however, something else in Groys' reconstruction that raises questions, namely the smoothness with which the avant-garde is absorbed into the *Gesamtkunstwerk* of Socialist Realism. The synthesis appears a bit too harmonious, as if the ghost of 'historical necessity' had suddenly reappeared on the stage (or rather, on the conductor's podium).

Admittedly, Groys' analysis – like this book – is concerned with the constructivist aspect of the avant-garde and pays little attention to its parodical and carnivalesque aspect, which in the 1920s flourished mainly in Leningrad (among the OBERIU poets, the director Igor Terentev, and others).[8] But even if many joined Mayakovsky in 'stepping on the throat of his own song' for the sake of social utility there was – as we have tried to show through the example of the theatre – plenty of provocative parody and semiotic experiment present in the 'leftist' avant-garde as well. This potentially dissonant element, however, is dismissed from Groys' synthesis in less than a sentence:

Revealed in this frivolous, irreverent play [of post-modernist *sots-art*] is that colossal potential of desire and the unconscious that was inherent in the Russian avant-garde but was insufficiently recognised because it was encoded in a rationalistic, geometric, technical, constructive form.[9]

Despite its evidential and rhetorical power, Boris Groys' conception of the 'birth of Socialist Realism from the spirit of the avant-garde' raises some questions. Were there no aspects of the avant-garde which could *not* enter Stalinist culture? Were there no contradictions within the aspects which *were* included? In the afterword to *Teatern som handling* in 1977 I attempted a very brief presentation of the avant-garde–Socialist Realist relationship which went beyond the then almost unanimously accepted antithetic version. One passage which proposed to answer at least the first of the above questions still seems valid.

The late 1920s found the avant-garde embroiled in a conflict with the so-called 'proletarian realists' (represented in literature and art by organisations with the impressive acronyms RAPP and AKhRR, later RAPKh). After having totally defeated the Party opposition, in 1928 Stalin introduced the first Five Year Plan and the building of 'socialism in one country'. At the same time, a violent polemics had erupted over the rôle of art and culture in this new utopian project which was basically a reiteration of the conflict between Proletkult and the avant-garde in the years of cultural revolution in 1918–20. As in the earlier debate, the Party initially assumed the position of an attentive observer while the majority of writers and artists without utopian inclinations remained silent (or were simply silenced by the censors). The specific programmes of the antagonists, however, had changed significantly. The 'proletarians' defended an 'intuitive' method (soon renamed 'dialectical-materialist') which implied the application of the classical realist forms of Tolstoy and Repin to contemporary themes. The avant-garde grouped around the journal *Novyi Lef* (*New Lef*, short for 'Left Front'), on the other hand, propagated 'factography', montage, and other forms recognisable as the 'minimum' programme of productionist aesthetics.[10]

The 'proletarian' spokesmen of realism in RAPP and AKhRR mechanically linked form and ideology – realism guaranteed 'correct ideology', and vice versa. The leftists, headed by Mayakovsky, Brik and Tretyakov, achieved brilliant polemical victories over the proponents of psychological proletarian realism, criticising them for holding on to obsolete forms and failing to incorporate technical advances ('the bourgeois novel in Red Army uniform'). The avant-garde itself, however, was actually trapped in a similar linking of technique and ideology. Unable to develop Mayakovsky's notion of 'the primacy of the goal over both form and content' in an undoctrinaire direction, the avant-gardists insisted on the applicability only of 'new' forms to socialist art, thus merely inverting RAPP's mechanical coupling of technique and ideology, form and content.[11]

It was not until the doctrine of Socialist Realism that 'the primacy of the goal over both form and content' was finally – and brutally – applied. To quote my own conclusions of 1977:

> The outcome of the struggle between the avant-garde and the advocates of 'proletarian realism' that came to a close with the First Congress of Writers in 1934 can be broadly summarised as follows.

The avant-garde's most interesting *technical* innovations in poetry, the visual arts, the theatre and the cinema were soon rejected as 'automatic' expressions of a decadent ideology. Important aspects of avant-garde *ideology*, on the other hand, met a peculiar and completely opposite fate. The intuitive and less than idealising 'dialectical method' in literature once advocated by RAPP was rejected in favour of a maximalist cult of power, expansion and heroism. Also in its view of the artist as a member of an élite chosen to lead the passive masses to a predetermined goal, Socialist Realism subscribes to the same Romantic notion of the *decisive and immediate social function of art* that exerted such a profound influence on the Russian avant-garde. Viewed from this perspective, Stalin's famous definition of writers as 'engineers of the human soul' seems to be a grim parody of the avant-garde technical bias transferred to the ideological realm.[12]

Thus I proposed to view Socialist Realism as a maximalist ideology in a realist costume, a synthesis whereby both the critical potential of realism and the technical innovations of the avant-garde were excluded. Groys comes very close to this interpretation, but he regards the 'realist' form as being determined by a general eclecticism (although, no doubt, this is its main representation):

Socialist Realism is usually defined as art which is 'socialist in content and national in form', but this also signifies 'avant-garde in content and eclectic in form', since by national is meant everything 'popular' and 'progressive' throughout the entire history of the nation.[13]

Rather like an anthropologist, in *Gesamtkunstwerk Stalin* Groys essays a reading of the evolution of the Russian avant-garde as one integral myth. In the present book the word 'myth' appears frequently but in a weaker sense, as in the 'myth of the representative audience'. This notion is shown to disintegrate when it is confronted by the spokesmen of 'reality' in the mid-1920s and exposed to the rationalist critique of Tretyakov (with its analogy in Brecht). In a similar way, a shift from the form/content opposition to the primacy of 'goal' (or reception) was foreseen in the late 1920s. Today, however, one might question the extent to which such demythologisation or enlightened criticism actually took place, or at least about its effects. The avant-garde itself was creating a myth which was used in turn as construction material for the Stalinist myth. Even the extreme rationalism of a Tretyakov had mythological (apocalyptic) traits, and in the building of Socialist Realism it was only its extremism that was utilised.[14]

The united and representative audience was a ready-made myth that was eminently well suited for incorporation into Socialist Realism, which denied in principle the existence of contradictions (other than with enemies of the people). It had only to be purged of its Wagnerian origins, which indeed was done in due course.[15]

Already in 1931, in the production of Vsevolod Vishnevsky's Red Navy melodrama *The Final Battle*, Meyerhold instrumentalised the notion of the united audience (almost in a 'ritual' form) to what he considered to be the demands of the day. In the tragic final scene, to the music of Scriabin's Sonata No. 3, he used a *claqueuse*, a woman placed in the stalls whose task it was to begin sobbing on a pre-arranged signal. And the audience wept along with her. Later yet another ending was added: the commander of the Soviet warship whose crew perished in 'the final battle' came out on stage and called upon everyone in the auditorium prepared to defend the Fatherland to stand up. Naturally, no one remained seated![16]

The critics were not pleased, however, and probably found that Meyerhold's patriotic ritual was excessively concerned with 'laying bare' a device which in the emerging Socialist Realist drama should instead be carefully concealed from the potential reflection of the spectator. At this stage in the construction of the new art – avant-garde maximalist in content but verisimilar in form – the psychological realism of the Moscow Art Theatre was much more in demand than the skills of Meyerhold. In the other arts, the situation was analogous. The 'demiurgic' contribution of the avant-garde project – the cultural revolution, the transformation of life by art, the creation of the New Man – was already in the process of being implemented on a new level. On the other hand, the formal aspect of avant-garde aesthetics – the insistence on function, on montage, on the destabilisation of meaning – would subsequently be denounced and suppressed.

Today, when a new, disillusioned enlightenment has apparently emerged victorious, the heritage of the Russian avant-garde might seem to have been totally exhausted, its utopianism consumed by totalitarianism, its formal experiment by post-modernism and/or commercialism. I think, however, that one should also consider such a view in its historical context. A decade from now, the rich heritage of the Russian avant-garde may well reappear before us in the different and unexpected light of novel interpretations to confront us with new questions.

Notes

Russian names in the text are given in a simplified form, but in the references below they are transliterated according to the *Slavonic Review* system.

Notes to Chapter 1

1. A detailed documentation of *October* is in Sergej Eisenstein, *Schriften*, vol. 3, ed. H. J. Schlegel (Munich, 1975). Cf. the analysis by Ö. Roth-Lindberg, 'Transformation as a Device in Eisenstein's Visual Language', in Lars Kleberg and Håkan Lövgren (eds), *Eisenstein Revisited. A Collection of Essays* (Stockholm, 1987), pp. 25–38.
2. See Mona Ozouf, *Festivals and the French Revolution*, trans. Alan Sheridan (Cambridge, Mass. and London, 1988) and A. Mazaev, *Prazdnik kak sotsial'no-khudozhestvennoe iavlenie* (Moscow, 1978).
3. 'Slap in the Face of Public Taste', in Anna Lawton (ed.), *Russian Futurism through its Manifestos, 1912–1928* (Ithaca and London, 1988), pp. 51–2.
4. The aesthetic theory of the Russian avant-garde in relation to earlier and later developments is analysed in Boris Groys, *Gesamtkunstwerk Stalin* (Munich, 1988) (translation into English by Charles Rougle, *The Total Art of Stalinism*, Princeton University Press, 1991); Groys develops the same argument in his 'The Birth of Socialist Realism from the Spirit of the Russian Avant-Garde', in Hans Günther (ed.), *The Culture of the Stalinist Period* (London, 1990), pp. 122–48. For the general theory of the autonomisation process and the avant-garde's subsequent project to abolish the institution of art, see Peter Burger, *Theory of the Avant-Garde*, trans. Michael Shaw (Manchester, 1984).
5. Cf. Richard Taylor, 'From October to *October*: the Soviet Political System and its Films', in M. J. Clark (ed.), *Politics and the Media* (Oxford, 1979), pp. 31–42.

Notes to Chapter 2

1. Sheila Fitzpatrick's *The Commissariat of Enlightenment* (Cambridge, 1970) still provides the best account of Lunacharsky's and Narkompros's activities in the immediate post-revolutionary period. On the conflicts in cultural policy during the first years of the revolution, see Nils Åke Nilsson (ed.), *Art, Society, Revolution: Russia 1917–1921* (Stockholm, 1979).
2. A. Lunacharskii, *Sobranie sochinenii*, vol. 7 (Moscow, 1967), p. 275.
3. Quoted in E. A. Dinershtein, 'Maiakovskii v fevrale–oktiabre 1917 g.', *Literaturnoe nasledstvo*, 65 (Moscow, 1956), p. 565.
4. Vladimir Maiakovskii, *Polnoe sobranie sochinenii*, vol. 12 (Moscow, 1959), p. 151.
5. Dinershtein, 'Maiakovskii v fevrale–oktiabre 1917 g.', p. 565.
6. The first non-partisan history of Proletkult as a national organisation is Lynn Mally, *Culture of the Future. The Proletkult Movement in Revolutionary Russia* (Berkeley, 1990). Most other studies on the Proletkult are strongly ideological. The Soviet historian V. V. Gorbunov criticises the movement for its left radicalism in *V. I. Lenin i proletkul't* (Moscow, 1974), whereas West German scholars praise it for those same tendencies; see P. Gorsen and E. Knödler-Bunte (eds), *Proletkult. Dokumentation* vols 1–2 (Stuttgart – Bad Canstatt, 1974). A dispassionate and informative account of Bogdanov's life and works is D. Grille, *Lenins Rivale* (Cologne, 1966). On the philosophical issues, see Zenovia A. Sochor, *Revolution and Culture: the Bogdanov–Lenin Controversy* (Ithaca, 1988).
7. Quoted in Gorsen and Knödler-Bunte, *Proletkult*, vol. 1, pp. 131–2.
8. Gorbunov, *V. I. Lenin i Proletkul't*, p. 59.
9. *Proletarskaia kul'tura*, 6 (1919), p. 35.
10. The project to found the '*komfuty*' ('communist-futurists') as a primary Party organisation in Petrograd was a rather pathetic attempt to assert the purely political significance of the avant-garde, and it was quickly dismissed by the Bolsheviks. See Bengt Jangfeldt, 'Russian Futurism 1917–1919', in Nilsson (ed.), *Art, Society, Revolution*, pp. 116–17.
11. 'Levye – pravye', *Isskustvo kommuny*, 3 (1918), p. 1.
12. Brik's 'Khudozhnik-proletarii' appeared in *Iskusstvo kommuny*, 2 (1918), p. 1. Cf. Masha Enzenberger's detailed presentation and translation of texts by Brik in *Screen*, 3 (1974), pp. 35–81. A pioneering typological study of the interrelation between the avant-garde, Proletkult and 'intuitive realism' in the 1920s is Miroslav Drozda and Milan Hrala, *Dvacátá léta sovětské literární kritiky (Lef – Rapp – Pereval)* (Prague, 1968).
13. V. I. Lenin, 'The Tax in Kind', *Collected Works*, vol. 32 (Moscow, 1965), p. 350. The economic and political crisis in Soviet Russia at the end of the Civil War is described in E. H. Carr, *The Bolshevik Revolution 1917–1923*, vols 1–3 (London, 1950–3) and Charles Bettelheim, *Class Struggle in the USSR* (New York, 1976). In *Revolutionary Dreams. Utopian Vision and Experimental Life in the Russian Revolution* (New York and Oxford, 1989), Richard Stites bases his description of a wide variety of utopian projects, including the Bolshevik one, on a wealth of primary and secondary sources. Mikhail Heller and Aleksandr Nekrich, *Utopia in Power. A*

History of the USSR from 1917 to the Present, trans. Phyllis B. Carlos (London, 1986), criticises the Bolshevik revolution as the utopia of totalitarianism and the destruction of culture as such.

14. Lenin, *Polnoe sobranie sochinenii*, vol. 32 (Moscow, 1965), p. 24 (my italics).
15. A. Kolontay, *The Workers' Opposition in Russia* (Chicago, 1921), p. 29. Cf. Mally, *Culture of the Future*, p. 195.
16. On the banning of Proletkult clubs, see Gorbunov, *V. I. Lenin i Proletkul't*, p. 172; on Proletkult and the Worker's Opposition see R. V. Daniels, *The Conscience of the Revolution* (Cambridge, Mass., 1960), pp. 159–61, and Mally, *Culture of the Future*, pp. 214–15.
17. Leo Trotsky, *Literature and Revolution*, trans. Rose Stunsky (Ann Arbor, 1960).
18. The speech at the Komsomol Congress is in Lenin, *Polnoe sobranie sochinenii*, vol. 31 (Moscow, 1966) pp. 283–99.
19. Kasimir Malevich, *Essays on Art*, ed. by Troels Andersen, trans. Xenia Glowacki-Prus and Arnold McMillin, vol. 1 (Copenhagen, 1968), p. 94. On the concept of the avant-garde in politics and the arts, see Donald D. Egbert, *Social Radicalism and the Arts. Western Europe* (New York, 1970), p. 117 ff.
20. 'Puti proletariata v izobrazitel'nom iskusstve', *Proletarskaia kul'tura*, 13–14 (1920), p. 73.
21. Anatoly Mazaev compares the situation to a pair of 'scissors' in which revolutionary enthusiasm was one blade, and material shortages and backwardness the other; the notion of production art was trapped in that scissors (A. Mazaev, *Kontseptsiia 'proizvodstvennogo iskusstva' 20-kh godov* (Moscow, 1975), p. 44). The standard work on constructivism and production art is Christina Lodder, *Russian Constructivism* (New Haven, 1983).
22. 'V poriadke dnia', *Iskusstvo i proizvodstvo*, 1 (Moscow, 1922), p. 7.
23. Maiakovskii, *Polnoe sobranie sochinenii*, vol. 12 (Moscow, 1959), p. 510.

Notes to Chapter 3

1. J. von Schlosser, 'Vom modernen Denkmalkultus', Vorträge der Bibliothek Warburg, 6 (Leipzig–Berlin 1926/1927), pp. 1–21.
2. Quoted from *Futurist Manifestos*, ed. and with an introduction by Umbro Apollonio (New York, 1973), p. 62.
3. 'Two Chekhovs' is in Maiakovskii, *Polnoe sobranie sochinenii*, vol. 1, pp. 294–301. For a discussion of Mayakovsky and the symbol of the statue, see Lars Kleberg, 'Notes on the Poem *Vladimir Il'ič Lenin*', in Bengt Jangfeldt and Nils Åke Nilsson (eds), *Vladimir Majakovskij. Memoirs and Essays* (Stockholm, 1975), pp. 166–78, and Krystyna Pomorska, 'Majakovskij and the Myth of Immortality in the Russian Avant-Garde', in Nils Åke Nilsson (ed.), *The Slavic Literatures and Modernism* (Stockholm, 1987), pp. 49–69.
4. *First Decrees of Soviet Power*, compiled and with explanatory notes by Yuri Akhapkin (London, 1970), p. 120.

5. For a full discussion of the project, see John Bowlt, 'Russian Sculpture and Lenin's Plan of Monumental Propaganda', in H. A. Millon and L. Nochlin (eds), *Art and Architecture in the Service of Politics* (Cambridge, Mass., 1978), pp. 182–93.

6. Quoted in Bengt Jangfeldt, 'Notes on "Manifest Letučej Federacii Futuristov" and the Revolution of the Spirit', in Jangfeldt and Nilsson (eds), *Vladimir Majakovskij*, p. 156.

7. Maiakovskii, *Polnoe sobranie sochinenii*, vol. 2, p. 16.

8. See Bengt Jangfeldt, *Majakovskij and Futurism 1917–1921* (Stockholm, 1976), pp. 51–2. On revolutionary iconoclasm in general, see Stites, *Revolutionary Dreams*, pp. 61–78.

9. 'Den', kotoryi my khotim khranit' v pamjati', *Iskusstvo kommuny*, 16 (1919), p. 1. On Punin, see Stites, *Revolutionary Dreams*, p. 50.

10. 'O pamiatnikakh', *Iskusstvo kommuny*, 14 (1919), pp. 2–3.

11. Tatlin's *Monument* is described in the catalogue of the Stockholm Museum of Modern Art (*Vladimir Tatlin. Moderna Museets utställningskatalog* [Stockholm, 1968]), in John Milner, *Vladimir Tatlin and the Russian Avant-Garde* (New Haven and London, 1983), and in Larissa Zhadova (ed.), *Tatlin* (London, 1988).

12. N. Punin, 'Monument to the III International', quoted in Zhadova, *Tatlin*, p. 345.

13. 'The Work Ahead of Us', in Zhadova, *Tatlin*, p. 239.

14. See A. M. Vogt, *Russische und französische Revolutionsarchitektur 1789–1917* (Cologne, 1974) and Lars Kleberg, 'Revolutionens symbolspråk i Frankrike och Tyskland', in Ronny Ambjörnsson and Sverker R. Ek (eds), *Franska revolutionen – bilder och myter* (Stockholm, 1989), pp. 89–108. John Milner (*Vladimir Tatlin and the Russian Avant-Garde*, pp. 176–80) points to the Pythagorean or 'astrological' aspects of Tatlin's tower, which only reinforce the parallel with French revolutionary architecture.

15. Maiakovskii, *Polnoe sobranie sochinenii*, vol. 2 (Moscow, 1957), pp. 149–65.

16. 'Too Early to Celebrate' is in Maiakovskii, *Polnoe sobranie sochinenii*, vol. 2 (Moscow, 1956), pp. 21–2. On the pseudo-religious character of Mayakovsky's poetry and utopian projects in Russia in general, see Andrei Sinyavsky, *Soviet Civilization*, trans. Joanne Turnbull with the assistance of Nikolai Formozov (New York, 1990), pp. 4–13.

17. Sergei Tret'iakov, *Itogo. Stikhi* (Moscow, 1924), pp. 8–9.

Notes to Chapter 4

1. Fritz Mierau's *Erfindung und Korrektur. Tretjakows Ästhetik der Operativität* (Berlin-DDR, 1976) is a valuable source of information, although it shows the strong imprint of the time and place of its publication.

2. The aesthetic revolution in the Russian theatre did not generate any new methodology in theatrical criticism paralleling formalism in the literary field. Although sympathetic and attentive to the work of Meyerhold and

the avant-garde, Professor Alexei Gvozdiev's Theatre Department at the State Institute for the History of the Arts in Leningrad (where the formalists dominated the Literature Department) was essentially eclectic and historical in its approach. On the development of the study of the theatre in Russia, see A. Ya. Altshuller et al. (eds), *Istoriia sovetskogo teatrovedeniia. Ocherki. 1917–1941* (Moscow, 1981). Theatre artists themselves were as always reluctant and/or unable to create a universal metalanguage for the analysis of their work. Sergey Eisenstein reports that his experience with Meyerhold as a teacher was traumatic, challenging him to create a general and complete theory for his chosen art, the cinema; see Eisenstein's essay 'Wie sag' ich's meinem Kind' ('And so. There you have it'), in his *Izbrannye proizvedeniia*, vol. 1 (Moscow, 1964), pp. 303–10 (English translation by Herbert Marshall in *Immoral Memories. An Autobiography by Sergei M. Eisenstein* (Boston and London, 1985), pp. 73–9). There is a vast literature on Eisenstein's cinematic theory, which was at once a 'superstructure' for his own works and an attempt to formulate the universals of (cinematic) art; see V. V. Ivanov, *Ocherki po istorii semiotiki v SSSR* (Moscow, 1976). For a 'translation' of Eisenstein's theory into the language of contemporary semiotics, see Herbert Eagle, 'Eisenstein as a Semiotician of the Cinema', in R. W. Bailey, L. Matejka and P. Steiner (eds), *The Sign: Semiotics around the World* (Ann Arbor, 1978), pp. 173–93.

Notes to Chapter 5

1. Tadeusz Kowzan, 'The Sign in the Theatre', *Diogenes*, 61 (1968), p. 73.
2. František Déak, 'Structuralism in the Theatre. The Prague School Contribution', *Drama Review*, 72 (December, 1976), pp. 83–94. For general introductions to the semiotics of theatre, see Erika Fischer-Lichte, *Semiotik des Theaters*, 1–3 (Tübingen, 1983), Keir Elam, *Semiotics of Theatre and Drama* (London, 1980), and Marvin Carlson, *Theatre Semiotics* (Bloomington and Indianapolis, 1990). Extensive bibliographies are in A. Van Kesteren and Herta Schmid (eds), *Moderne Dramentheorien* (Kronberg/ Ts., 1975), pp. 318–88, and A. Van Kesteren and Herta Schmid (eds), *Semiotics of Drama and Theatre* (Amsterdam and Philadelphia, 1984), pp. 511–48. Susan Bennett's *Theatre Audiences. A Theory of Production and Reception* (London and New York, 1990) is the first book-length survey on the subject. On the definition of the limits of theatrical art, specifically in the light of happening aesthetics, see Rolf Schäfer, *Ästhetisches Handeln als Kategorie einer interdisziplinaren Theaterwissenschaft* (Aachen, 1988), pp. 133–46, 202–26 (bibliography, pp. 334–59).
3. Jan Mukařovský, 'On the Current State of the Theory of Theatre', in *Structure, Sign, and Function. Selected Essays by Jan Mukařovský*, trans. and ed. John Burbank and Peter Steiner (New Haven and London, 1978), pp. 201–19; quotation on pp. 207–8.
4. Olle Hildebrand, *Harlekin Frälsaren. Teater och verklighet i Nikolaj Evreinovs dramatik* (Uppsala, 1978), p. 14.

5. Bertolt Brecht, 'A Short Organon for the Theatre', in *Brecht on Theatre. The Development of an Aesthetic*, ed. and trans. John Willett (London, 1964), p. 181.
6. Iu. M. Lotman, *Stat'i po tipologii kult'tury*, 2 (Tartu, 1973), p. 42. An English translation of this article is 'Theater and Theatricality in the Order of Early Nineteenth-Century Culture', in Henryk Baran (ed.), *Semiotics and Structuralism* (White Plains, NY, 1976), pp. 33–63; quotation on p. 33. See also Iu. M. Lotman, 'Semiotika stseny', *Teatr* no. 1 (1980), pp. 89–99.
7. Mukařovský, 'On the Current State of the Theory of Theatre', p. 201.
8. Jonas Barish, *The Anti-theatrical Prejudice* (Berkeley, 1981) is a fascinating history of the attacks on the boundaries between 'theatre' and 'life' (on Rousseau, see pp. 256–94). Russian examples, however, fall outside the scope of the book.
9. Richard Wagner, *Art and Revolution*, in *Richard Wagner's Prose Works*, trans. William Ashton Ellis, vol. 1 (New York, 1966), p. 34.
10. *Art and Revolution* was translated into Russian in 1906. On Wagner and the Russian artistic intelligentsia, see Bernice Glatzer Rosenthal, 'Wagner and Wagnerian Ideas in Russia', in D. Large and W. Weber (eds), *Wagnerism in European Culture and Politics* (Ithaca, 1984), pp. 198–245.
11. Quoted in Martin Esslin, *Mediations* (London, 1980), p. 18.
12. Julius Bab, 'Idee und Aufgabe der Volksbühne', in *Wesen und Weg der Berliner Volksbühnebewegung* (Berlin, 1919), p. 1.
13. Bernard Dort, *Théâtre réel* (Paris, 1971), p. 269.
14. Romain Rolland, *Théâtre du peuple* (Paris, 1903). First Russian edn. *Narodnyi teatr* (St Petersburg, 1910). English edn, *The People's Theatre*, trans. Barret H. Clark (London, 1918). See also David Bradbury and James McCormick, *People's Theatre*, (London, 1978) and David James Fisher, 'Romain Rolland and the French People's Theatre', *Drama Review*, 73 (March 1977), pp. 75–90.

Notes to Chapter 6

1. The typological analysis attempted here is based on existing historical descriptions and meta-descriptions by the directors and theoreticians mentioned in the text. For the purpose of the argument, exemplification is limited to the best known facts. Readers interested in a full and complex historical description of the factual material on which my reconstruction is based are addressed to Konstantin Rudnitsky's magnificently illustrated *Russian and Soviet Theatre. Tradition and the Avant-Garde*, trans. Roxane Permar (London, 1988). See also the reprint of the classical survey from the 1920s, René Fueloep-Miller and Joseph Gregor, *The Russian Theatre. Its Character and History with a Special Reference to the Revolutionary Period*, trans. Paul England (New York, 1968).
2. Reprinted in Valerii Bryusov, *Sobranie sochinenii*, vol. 6 (Moscow, 1975), pp. 62–73. The arguments were summarised in Bryusov's contribution to the 1908 anthology *Teatr. Kniga o novom teatre*, translated as 'Realism

and Convention on the Stage', in Laurence Senelick (ed.), *Russian Dramatic Theory from Pushkin to the Symbolists* (Austin, 1981), pp. 171–82.
3. Friedrich Nietzsche, *The Birth of Tragedy and The Case of Wagner*, trans. and ed. Walter Kaufman (New York, 1967), p. 37.
4. V. I. Ivanov, *Po zvezdam. Stat'i i aforizmy* (St Petersburg, 1909; reprint, Letchworth, 1971) and *Borozdy i mezhi* (St Petersburg, 1916; reprint, Letchworth, 1971). Ivanov's programmatic essay 'The Theatre of the Future' was translated as early as 1912 in *English Review*, 10 (March 1912), pp. 634–50; the more philological 'The Essence of Tragedy' is included in Senelick (ed.), *Russian Dramatic Theory*, pp. 210–22. For general introductions to Ivanov, whose importance for both pre- and post-revolutionary aesthetic and philosophic thought in Russia has only recently been generally acknowledged, see James West, *Russian Symbolism. A Study of Vyacheslav Ivanov and the Russian Symbolist Aesthetic* (London, 1970), and Robert Louis Jackson and Lowry Nelson Jr (eds), *Vyacheslav Ivanov: Poet, Critic, and Philosopher* (New Haven, 1986). On Ivanov's theatrical utopia, see Lars Kleberg, 'Vjačeslav Ivanov and the Idea of Theatre', in Lars Kleberg and Nils Åke Nilsson (eds), *Theatre and Literature in Russia 1900–1930* (Stockholm, 1984), pp. 57–70. Cf. also Chapter 11, note 7 below. On Scriabin's utopian works, to which Ivanov often refers, see James H. Billington, *The Icon and the Axe. An Interpretative History of Russian Culture* (New York, 1966), pp. 481–4.
5. Lars Kleberg, 'Sootnoshenie stseny i zritel'nogo zala. K tipologii russkogo teatra nachala XX veka', *Scando-Slavica*, 20 (1974), pp. 27–38. Yevreinov's aesthetics are summarised in Nicholas Evreinov, *The Theatre in Life*, ed. and trans. Alexander Nazaroff (London, 1927). I am indebted to Olle Hildebrand for his analysis of Yevreinov in *Harlekin Frälsaren* and for helpful comments and criticism. See his comparison of Yevreinov's 'theatre-in-life' with Pirandello's aesthetics, 'Pirandello's Theatre and the Influence of Nicolai Evreinov', *Italica*, 60 (Summer 1983), pp. 107–39.
6. On the pre-revolutionary people's theatre movement, see G. A. Khaichenko, *Russkii narodnyi teatr kontsa XIX–nachala XX veka* (Moscow, 1975) and Gary Thurston's 'The Impact of Russian Popular Theatre, 1886–1915', *Journal of Modern History*, 55 (June 1983), pp. 237–67, and 'Theatre and Acculturation in Russia from Peasant Emancipation to the First World War', *Journal of Popular Culture*, 18 (Fall 1984), pp. 3–16. The writer Yevgeny Zamyatin remarked sarcastically that this people's theatre was 'a kind of subtheatre, in which there is nothing left of the people, its tastes, or its language, a theatre made by the upper classes for the lower' (*Blokha. Igra v 4 akta Evgeniia Zamiatina. Sbornik statei* (Leningrad, 1927), p. 4).
7. See Lars Kleberg, '"People's Theatre" and the Revolution', in Nilsson (ed.), *Art, Society, Revolution*, pp. 179–97; Bernice Glatzer Rosenthal, 'Theatre as Church: The Vision of the Mystical Anarchists', *Russian History*, 4, pt. 2 (1977), pp. 122–41.
8. Ivanov, *Po zvezdam* (Petersburg, 1908), pp. 218–19.
9. *Teatr. Kniga o novom teatre* (St Petersburg, 1908), p. 272. Bely's article is translated as 'Theatre and Modern Drama' in Senelick (ed.), *Russian Dramatic Theory*, pp. 149–70. The (somewhat differently worded) quotations are on pp. 158–9.

10. Meyerhold notes that here he is quoting a letter from the writer Leonid Andreyev; his article is translated in *Meyerhold on Theatre*, trans. and ed. Edward Braun (London, 1969); quotation on p. 63.
11. *Krizis teatra* (Moscow, 1908). See also the poet Alexander Blok's 1908 essay 'O teatre', in his *Sobranie sochinenii*, vol. 5 (Moscow–Leningrad, 1962), pp. 241–76.
12. Rikhard Vagner, *Iskusstvo i revoliutsiia* (Petrograd, 1918); Lunacharsky's introduction is on p. 1. – Romen Rollan, *Narodnyi teatr* (Petrograd–Moscow, 1919), foreword by Vyacheslav Ivanov, pp. vii–xv. The ideas of pre-revolutionary people's theatre were propagated by V. Tikhonovich, *Narodnyi teatr*, 1–2 (Moscow, 1918) and the journal he edited, *Narodnyi teatr* (three issues published in 1918: nos. 1, 2, and 3–4).
13. On Vakhtangov's People's Theatre project, see Nick Worrall, *Modernism to Realism on the Soviet Stage: Tairov – Vakhtangov – Okhlopkov* (Cambridge, 1989), pp. 100–1; Worrall's book contains valuable information that has not been readily available in Western sources.
14. P. Kerzhentsev, *Tvorcheskii teatr* (Petrograd, 1918). Subsequent editions in Petrograd (1919), Moscow (1919), Petersburg (1920), Moscow (1923); in German, *Das schöpferische Theater* (Hamburg, 1922), and a new edition with a postcript by Richard Weber (Cologne, 1980). Kerzhensev's book was immediately adopted by Proletkult and the left but was reviewed as 'Creative Theatre, or an Apology for the Triumphant Lack of Talent' in the leading theatrical journal of the preceding decade, *Teatr i Iskusstvo*, 24–25 (1918), pp. 251–4. Despite the vehement protests of its editor, the brilliant critic Alexander Kugel, the journal was soon afterwards closed down.
15. Alexander Tairov, *Notes of a Director*, trans. William Kuhlke (Coral Gables, Fla., 1969), pp. 132–43. On Tairov, see Rudnitsky, *Russian and Soviet Theatre*, *passim*, and Worrall, *Modernism to Realism on the Soviet Stage*, pp. 15–75.
16. *Tvorcheskii teatr* (Petersburg, 1920), p. 88.
17. For descriptions of revolutionary mass spectacles, see V. Rafalovich (ed.), *Istoriia sovetskogo teatra*, 1 (Leningrad, 1933), pp. 264–90; Vladimir Tolstoy, Irina Bibikova and Catherine Cook (eds), *Street Art of the Revolution* (London, 1990); A. Mazaev, *Prazdnik kak sotsial'no-khudozhestvennoe iavlenie* (Moscow, 1978), pp. 235–300; František Déak, 'Russian Mass Spectacles', *Drama Review*, 66 (June 1975), pp. 8–22; Robert Russell, 'People's Theatre and the Revolution', *Irish Slavonic Studies*, 7 (1986), pp. 65–84; and James von Geldern, *Festivals of the Revolution, 1917–1920: Art and Theater in the Formation of Soviet Culture* (forthcoming).
18. *Pervyi vserossiiskii s"ezd po raboche-krest'ianskomu teatru 17–26 noiabria 1919* (Moscow, 1920); A. Iufit (ed.), *Sovetskii teatr. Dokumenty i materialy: Russkii sovetskii teatr 1917–1921* (Leningrad, 1968), pp. 76ff. The argument that Ivanov and other symbolist writers who worked in the Theatre Section of Narkompros formed a kind of anti-Soviet resistance group is clearly the product of Cold War historiography. It is evident, for example, in Nikolai A. Gorchakov, *The Theater in Soviet Russia* (New York, 1957), pp. 115–16, which nevertheless deserves to be noted for what at the time

was a uniquely detailed presentation of directors and tendencies in the
Soviet Russian theatre of the 1920s and 1930s.

19. *Vestnik teatra*, 26 (1919), p. 4. Writing in 1917–18, Fyodor Sologub,
another symbolist contributor to the anthology *Teatr*. *Kniga o novom
teatre* (1908), also expressed hopes for a revival of the people's theatre
based on the creation of a new myth: 'Teatr – khram', *Teatr i Iskusstvo*, 3
(1917), pp. 50–2; 'Nabliudeniia i mechty o teatre', *Russkaia mysl'*, 1–2
(1918), pp. 1–20. In 1922 V. V. Gippius made a more self-critical evaluation of the prerevolutionary intelligentsia's utopia ('Teatr i narod', in K.
Erberg (ed.), *Iskusstvo staroe i novoe*, 1 [Petersburg, 1921], pp. 86–93).
20. Rafalovich (ed.), *Istoriia sovetskogo teatra*, p. 259.
21. See Rudnitsky, *Russian and Soviet Theatre*, pp. 44–5, 68–9; quotation
from Bernard Dort, *Théâtre public* (Paris, 1967), p. 366.
22. The phrase is borrowed from Joachim Paech, *Das Theater der russischen
Revolution* (Kronberg/Ts., 1974), p. 288.

Notes to Chapter 7

1. Meyerhold's work of the early 1920s is analysed in Konstantin Rudnitsky,
Meyerhold the Director, trans. George Petrov (Ann Arbor, 1981); Marjorie
Hoover, *Meyerhold: The Art of Conscious Theatre* (Amherst, 1974); Eduard
Braun, *The Theatre of Meyerhold. Revolution on the Modern Stage* (New
York and London, 1979); Christian Mailand-Hansen, *Mejerchol'ds
Theaterästetik in den 1920er Jahren* (Copenhagen, 1980); Robert Leach,
Vsevolod Meyerhold (Cambridge, 1989); and Beatrice Picon-Vallin,
Meyerhold (Paris, 1990).
2. *Meyerhold on Theatre*, pp. 170–1.
3. Quoted from Rudnitsky, *Meyerhold the Director*, pp. 272–3.
4. Vsevolod Meierkhol'd, *Stat'i, pis'ma, rechi, besedy*, vol. 2 (Moscow,
1968), p. 14.
5. Meierkhol'd, *Stat'i, pis'ma, rechi, besedy*, vol. 2, p. 485.
6. On Gastev, see A. Mazaev, *Kontseptsiia 'proizvodstvennogo iskusstva'
20-kh godov* (Moscow, 1975), pp. 60–9; Kurt Johansson, *Aleksej Gastev.
Proletarian Bard of the Machine Age* (Stockholm, 1983), pp. 104–5; and
Stites, *Revolutionary Dreams*, pp. 145–64.
7. *Meyerhold on Theatre*, p. 197.
8. On biomechanics, see Picon-Vallin, *Meyerhold*, *passim*; Mel Gordon,
'Meyerhold's Biomechanics', *Drama Review*, 63 (September 1974), pp.
73–88; Nick Worrall, 'Meyerhold's "The Magnificent Cuckold"', *Drama
Review*, 57 (March 1973), pp. 14–34; Alma Law, 'Meyerhold's "The
Magnanimous Cuckold"', *Drama Review*, 93 (March 1982), pp. 61–86;
Alma Law, 'The Death of Tarelkin: A Constructivist Vision of Tsarist
Russia', *Russian History*, 8, pts 1–2 (1981), pp. 145–98. On the relation of
biomechanics to circus and *commedia dell'arte*, see Picon-Vallin,
Meyerhold, pp. 125–40. Edward Braun, whose approach to Meyerhold is
essentially comparativistic, is sceptical towards the 'scientific' aspects of
biomechanics: *The Theatre of Meyerhold*, p. 68.

9.   Ivan Aksenov, 'Prostranstvennyi konstruktivizm na stsene', *Teatral'nyi Oktiabr'*, 1 (Leningrad–Moscow, 1926) p. 33.

10. On the analogous tension between 'aesthetic' and 'documentary' in Russian literature at the same time, see Peter Alberg Jensen, 'Art – Artifact – Fact: The Set on "Reality" in the Prose of the 1920s', in Nils Åke Nilsson (ed.), *The Slavic Literatures and Modernism* (Stockholm, 1987), pp. 113–25.

11. Christine Hamon, 'La terre cabrée', in *Les voies de la création théâtral*, 7 (Paris, 1979), pp. 45–60. The quotation is from S. Tretyakov, 'Zemlia dybom. Tekst i rechemontazh', *Zrelishcha*, no. 27 (1923), p. 6 (my italics).

12. Meierkhol'd, *Stat'i*, vol. 2, p. 52.

13. S. Tret'iakov, 'Vsevolod Meierkhol'd', *Lef*, 2 (1923), p. 169.

14. Boris Arvatov, 'Teatr, kak proizvodstvo', in *O teatre* (Tver', 1922), pp. 113–22; quotation on p. 115. German trans. by Hans Günther in Boris Arvatov, *Kunst und Produktion* (Munich, 1972), pp. 85–92.

15. Marinetti's 'Variety Theatre Manifesto' (1913) had been translated into Russian already before the First World War under the title 'Music Hall' in *Manifesty ital'ianskogo futurizma*, ed. and trans. Vadim Shershenevich (Moscow, 1914), pp. 72–7. See A. Ripellino, *Majakovskij und das russische Theater der Avantgarde* (Cologne, 1964), p. 163ff.; Håkan Lövgren, 'Sergej Radlov's Electric Baton: The "Futurization" of Russian Theater', in Kleberg and Nilsson (eds), *Theatre and Literature in Russia 1900–1930*, pp. 101– 13; and Rudnitsky, *Russian and Soviet Theatre*, pp. 94–9. A special section is devoted to eccentrism in *Drama Review*, 68 (December 1975), pp. 88–123, with translations of texts by Konzintsev, Trauberg, Radlov, et al.

16. Meierkhol'd, *Stat'i*, vol. 2, pp. 28–9.

17. Arvatov, 'Teatr, kak proizvodstvo', pp. 121–2. Considering the connection of the Proletkult movement with the trade-union opposition (see above, pp. 20–1), it is noteworthy that when Arvatov's articles were reprinted in his book *Ob agitatsionnom i proizvodstvennom iskusstve* (Moscow, 1930), there was one point in the long list that was missing: *strikes*.

Notes to Chapter 8

1.   Sergei Eisenstein, 'The Montage of Attractions', in his *Selected Works*, vol. 1, trans. and ed. Richard Taylor (London and Indiana, 1988), p. 34. The present translation is somewhat closer to the original.

2.   The most comprehensive account of the facts remains Alexander Fevral'skii, 'S. M. Eizenshtein v teatre', in *Voprosy teatra 1967* (Moscow, 1968), pp. 82–101; see also Daniel Gerould, 'Eisenstein's Wise Man', *Drama Review*, 61 (March 1974), pp. 77–88, and Tadeusz Szczepański, 'The Wise Man Reconsidered: Some Notes on the Performance', in Kleberg and Lövgren (eds), *Eisenstein Revisited*, pp. 11–24.

3.   The FEKS ('Factory of the Eccentric Actor') production was satirised – evidently without great exaggeration – in I. Ilf and E. Petrov's famous picaresque novel of the 1920s, *The Twelve Chairs*, trans. John H. C.

Richardson (New York, 1961), ch. XXX, 'In the Columbus Theater'.

4. Sergei Tret'iakov, *Slyshish', Moskva?!* – *Protivogazy* – *Rychi, Kitai!* (Moscow, 1966), pp. 3–28. English translation by Liudmilla Hirsch in *Drama Review*, 79 (September 1978), pp. 113–23.

5. Tretyakov's text was intended as a propaganda play to enlist volunteers for the expected (but never realised) revolution in Germany in the autumn of 1923. On different forms of dramaturgical involvement of the audience, see Volker Klotz, *Dramaturgie des Publikums* (Munich, 1976).

6. S. Tret'iakov, 'Teatr attraktsionov', *Oktiabr' mysli*, 1 (1924), pp. 53–6; the quotations are on p. 54. See also Tretyakov's 'Rabochii teatr', *Oktiabr' mysli*, 5–6, pp. 53–8.

7. S. M. Eizenshtein, *Izbrannye prizvedeniia*, vol. 1 (Moscow, 1964), p. 104.

8. On reflexology in Eisenstein's early work, see T. Selezneva, *Kinomysl' 1920-kh godov* (Leningrad, 1972), p. 105ff.

9. Eisenstein, *Selected Works*, vol. 1, p. 65.

10. Tretyakov also devoted considerable attention to the composition of the audience. In the article 'The Theatre of Attractions' (pp. 5–6) he declared that the attractions must be tested

> in relation to a particular audience (otherwise the effect will be spurious and non-uniform) . . . . The theatre of attractions can only be structured upon an audience with a stable class basis, and it must regard that audience as material that is to be shaped in a particular way.

In the same article, Tretyakov discussed the concrete results of the Proletkult Theatre's experiments in influencing the audience. He was forced to admit that the political satire and agitation in *The Wiseman* had been thrust deep into the background. Despite its technical brilliance and the response that the clowning evoked in the audience, *The Wiseman* was a purely experimental production that was 'as non-figurative as [Meyerhold's] *The Cuckold*'. *Do You Hear, Moscow?!* was a more successful 'processing of the spectators' emotions'. True, the failure of the revolution in Germany to materialise deprived the work of some of its desired effect. More serious in Tretyakov's view, however, was the fact that the audience had had a faulty, much too heterogeneous class composition:

> The production corresponded 70 per cent to the original calculation. Not 100 per cent, because (1) historical events robbed the play of some of its direct intent, and (2) with respect to class composition the spectators were far from the homogeneous audience that the Theatre of Attractions should seek to influence, and that must be analysed if maximum effect is to be achieved.

11. For example, Peter Wollen, *Signs and Meaning in Cinema* (London, 1972), pp. 37–9.

12. Eizenshtein, *Izbrannye proizvedeniia*, vol. 5 (Moscow, 1968), p. 52.

13. On 17 April 1924, one more performance of *The Gas Masks* was given on the regular stage of the Proletkult Theatre in the centre of the city, and another three stagings were arranged in the centre the following season before the play closed down. Thus there were never more than eight performances of Eisenstein's production, and of these only four took place

at the gas works. If these figures are compared with those for *The Wiseman* (52 performances) and *Do You Hear, Moscow?!* (57), *The Gas Masks* appears to be a mere experiment, all the more so if it is considered that the proletarian audience (10,000 workers in the Kursk district), whose reactions the author and director claimed they wanted to test, hardly had a chance to see the performance. Facts about the Proletkult Theatre's repertory are taken from the two Moscow theatrical journals *Novyi zritel'* and *Zrelishcha* of 1924. A. Trabskii (ed.), *Sovetskii teatr. Dokumenty i materialy: Russkii sovetskii teatr 1921–1926* (Leningrad, 1975), p. 273, mentions a total of only six performances of *The Gas Masks*.

14.   My play *The Sorcerer's Apprentices* is a fictitious reconstruction of a discussion of Mei Lan-fang's performances among these and other directors; see Lars Kleberg, *Stjärnfall. En triptyk* (Stockholm and Lund, 1988), pp. 37–75; French edn, *La chute des étoiles*, trans. Katarzyna Skansberg (Paris, 1990), pp. 45–86; English edn forthcoming. The minutes from a 1935 public discussion with Mei Lan-fang in Moscow in which Meyerhold and Eisenstein did take part has recently been discovered in a Russian archive (published with an introduction by Lars Kleberg, 'Zhivye impul'sy iskusstva', *Iskusstvo kino*, 1 (1992), pp. 132–9).

15.   *The Times* (London), 7 July 1924, p. 13, reproduced in Tretjakow, *Brülle, China! – Ich will ein Kind haben*, trans. Fritz Mierau (Berlin-DDR, 1976), p. 40. Cf. Myong Ja Jung-Baek, *S. Tret'jakov und China* (Göttingen, 1987).

16.   S. Tret'iakov, *Slyshish', Moskva?! – Protivogazy – Rychi, Kitai!* (Moscow, 1966), pp. 63–153; English edn *Roar, China!* trans. F. Polianovska and Barbara Nixon (New York, 1931).

17.   Eizenshtein, *Izbrannye proizvedeniia*, vol. 3 (Moscow, 1964), p. 46. Cf. Caniel Gerould, 'Historical Simulation and Popular Entertainment: The *Potemkin* Mutiny from Reconstructed Newsreel to *Black Sea Stuntmen'*, *Drama Review*, 122 (Summer 1989), pp. 161–84.

18.   Lars Kleberg, 'Ejzenštejn's *Potemkin* and Tret'jakov's *Ryči, Kitaj!*, *Scando-Slavica*, 23 (1977), pp. 29–37.

19.   Rudnitsky, *Russian and Soviet Theatre*, pp. 197–8.

20.   Fritz Mierau, 'Tatsache und Tendenz', in S. Tretjakow, *Lyrik – Dramatik – Prosa* (Leipzig, 1972), pp. 471–6.

Notes to Chapter 9

1.   This chapter is an abbreviated version of my article 'The Nature of the Soviet Audience', in Robert Russell and Andrew Barratt (eds), *Russian Theatre in the Age of Modernism* (London, 1990), pp. 172–95.

2.   H. Kindermann and M. Dietrich (eds), *Das Theater und sein Publikum. Referate der Internationalen theaterwissenschaftlichen Dozentenkonferenzen in Venedig 1975 und Wien 1976* (Vienna, 1977) gives an overview of current approaches and the still elementary level of research in the field until the 1970s. For a survey of later developments, see the special issue 'Le rôle du spectateur' of the French journal *Théâtre public*, 55 (1984), and Marco de Marini, 'Dramaturgy of the Spectator', *Drama*

Review, 114 (Summer 1987), pp. 100–14 (with bibliography). In none of these is there any mention of the Soviet Russian experience of the 1920s.

3. The only researchers who, to my knowledge, have dealt with this topic approach it exclusively from the point of view of the development of Soviet theatrical sociology, leaving unconsidered the question of its relationship to the theatrical practice of the mid-1920s. See V. Dmitrievskii, 'O konkretno-sotsiologicheskom izuchenii teatral'nogo zritelia', in *Teatr i dramaturgiia*, vol. 2 (Leningrad, 1967), pp. 146–69, and 'Nekotorye voprosy metodiki izucheniia interesov i reaktsii teatral'nogo zritelia', in *Khudozhestvennoe vospriatie. Sbornik I* (Leningrad, 1971), pp. 366–85; see also L. I. Novozhilova and I. L. Nosova, 'Teatr i zritel'', in *Nauka o teatre. Mezhvuzovskii sbornik* (Leningrad, 1975), pp. 418–34; N. A. Khrenov, 'Sotstiologicheskie i sotsial'no-psikhologicheskie mekhanizmy formirovaniia publiki', in *Voprosy sotsiologii iskusstva* (Leningrad, 1980), pp. 59–75; and A. Kulkin et at. (eds), *Iskusstvo i obshchenie* (Leningrad, 1984).

4. M. Zagorskii, 'Kak reagiruet zritel'?' *Lef*, no. 2 (6) (1924), pp. 141–51; quotation on pp. 141–2.

5. Zagorskii, 'Kak reagiruet zritel'?' p. 142.

6. In fact, this was not the first time such polls were used in the Russian theatre. In September and early October 1917 the so-called Mobile Public Theatre from Petrograd, led by P. P. Gaideburov and N. F. Skarskaia, toured the front and had their soldier audiences fill in questionnaires. For an interesting description of these, see A. A. Bardovskii, *Teatral'nyi zritel' na fronte v kanun Oktiabria* (Leningrad, 1928). Zagorskii first presented his audience studies of 1920–1 in the article 'Teatr i zritel' epokhi revoliutsii' in *O teatre* (Tver', 1922), pp. 102–12.

7. Questionnaires from the other famous production of the RSFSR Theatre no. 1, *Dawn*, are preserved in the archive of the Meyerhold theatre in the Central State Archive of Literature and Art in Moscow: TsGALI, f. 963, op. 1, ed. khr. 9.

8. Zagorskii, 'Kak reagiruet zritel'?' p. 151.

9. V. Fedorov, 'Opyty izucheniia zritel'nogo zala', *Zhizn' iskusstva* (referred to as *ZhI* below) no. 18 (1925), pp. 14–15.

10. Fedorov, 'Opyty izucheniia', p. 14.

11. Copies of pre-printed, double-folio format charts with the heading *List VII. Uchet reaktsii zritel'nogo zala* ('Chart VII. Account of Audience Reactions') are preserved in the Meyerhold theatre archive in TsGALI, f. 963, op. 1, ed. khr. 1048. The complete list of standard reactions with code numbers is as follows: (1) Silence. (2) Noises. (3) Great noise. (4) Reading in chorus [probably the audience following the text by reading aloud]. (5) Singing. (6) Coughing. (7) Stamping. (8) Clearing throats. (9) Exclamations. (10) Weeping. (11) Laughter. (12) Sighs. (13) Commotion. (14) Applause. (15) Whistling. (16) Hushing. (17) Leaving the auditorium. (18) Rising from seats. (19) Throwing objects on to the stage. (20) Climbing on to the stage.

12. Fedorov, 'Opyty izucheniia', p. 15.

13. M. Zagorskii, 'Esche ob izuchenii zritelia', *ZhI*, no. 20 (1925), pp. 5–6; quotation on p. 5.

14. A. Gvozdev, 'Zritel' i ego issledovateli', *ZhI*, no. 22 (1925), p. 6.
15. V. Fedorov, 'Opyty izucheniia zritel'nogo zala. II', *ZhI*, no. 23 (1925), pp. 10–11.
16. This concept was introduced on the analogy of the Taylor system in industry.
17. It is doubtful whether such complete records of the performances at the Meyerhold theatre were ever kept as systematically as Fyodorov implies. The documentation available in the archive of the theatre in TsGALI is in fact scanty. Of the twenty-one charts of the type mentioned above in note 11 from the performances of *Bubus the Teacher* in the spring season of 1925, for example, some were filled in by two different assistants covering the same performance (f. 963, op. 1, ed. khr. 1048). The charts often have only a few notes on them or have been left incomplete; not surprisingly, the most detailed charts are those countersigned by the future chronicler of the theatre and editor of Meyerhold's writings, the infallibly accurate Alexander Fevralsky. Only three of these twenty-one charts contain any information about the composition of the audience (*sostav zritel'nogo zala*): in one case all the tickets had been taken by a group of Young Pioneers, while in the other two there is a note stating that the auditorium was only one-half or one-third full. In TsGALI there are charts of the same type relating to at least two more productions: 131 charts with very few notes from Erdman's *Mandate*, May–December 1925 (f. 963, op. 1, ed. khr. 1049) and from the dress rehearsals and opening night of the famous production of Gogol's *Government Inspector*, 7–9 December 1926 (f. 963, op. 1, ed. khr. 1050). These 'Accounts of Audience Reactions' on the large form No. VII were theoretically to be accompanied by six other smaller and less detailed charts, copies of which are also preserved: I. Staff; II. *Khronometrazh*; III. Intermissions; IV. Actors; V. Stage Hands; VI. Box Office and Administration. As far as I can judge from the material made available to me in TsGALI, these other charts were only used sporadically to supplement Chart VII.
18. As a matter of fact, questionnaires *were* used at this time by the Meyerhold theatre parallel to the 'objective' research project. In TsGALI (f. 963, op. 1, ed. khr. 918) there are 188 questionnaires from the theatre's guest performance of Ostrovsky's *The Forest* in Ivanovo-Voznesensk in March 1925. Under the heading 'What do you think about "The Forest"? Question Form', the following questions were asked: (1) 'Have you seen "The Forest" in other theatres?' (2) 'Where do you think "The Forest" was staged the best?' (3) 'What was the difference?' (4) 'Was "The Forest" as we staged it an agitational play?' (5) 'Did you find the performance tiring? (If so, state why.)' (6) 'Do you have any further comments?' In addition the respondent was asked to state sex, age, profession, trade union and party affiliation. The purpose of this questionnaire and another one done in 1928 (f. 963, op. 1, ed. khr. 919) was evidently to help the theatre evaluate its guest performance in towns outside Moscow. The questionnaires concerning the 1920 production of *Dawn* mentioned above in note 7 and later polls are awaiting further research.
19. A. Bardovskii, 'Izuchenie zritelia', *ZhI*, no. 23 (1925), p. 16; M. Zagorskii, 'Diskussiia o zritele prodolzhaetsia', *ZhI*, no. 26 (1925), pp. 12–13; V.

Fedorov, 'Diskussiia o zritele', *ZhI*, no. 27 (1925), p. 9.
20. See note 6 above.
21. On audience research in children's theatre, see Kleberg, 'The Nature of the Soviet Audience', pp. 184–7.
22. M. Zagorskii, 'Kak izuchat' zritelia', *Novyi zritel'*, no. 28 (1925), p. 8.
23. For evidence that this approach was never totally abandoned by Meyerhold and that at times – not without a measure of cynicism – it could be applied successfully, see the Postscript below, p. 126.
24. T. Cole and H. K. Chinoy (eds), *Directors on Directing* (Indianapolis–New York, 1963), p. 53.

Notes to Chapter 10

1. Sergei Tret'iakov, *Khochu rebenka* (1-i variant), *Sovremennaia dramaturgiia*, no. 2 (1988), pp. 209–37; quotation on p. 213.
2. Soviet sociologist S. G. Strumilin's classic 1926 study *Rabochii byt v tsifrakh* (in his *Izbrannye proizvedeniia*, 3 (Moscow, 1964), pp. 250–74) provides striking figures on the living conditions of the Russian worker in 1924: out of 100 workers' families (averaging 4 members), less than 50 had bedsheets, 68.9 had a pair of scissors, 25 had a shaving knife; on the average there was 1 towel per 2–3 persons and 1 watch per family.
3. There just might be a hidden self-portrait of Tretyakov here, although it is uncertain whether he would have consciously permitted himself such a frivolity. For a discussion of the structure of the play, see Eduard Ditschek, *Politisches Engagement und Medienexperiment* (Tübingen, 1989), pp. 183–94, and especially *idem*, 'Attraktionsmontage und Diskussionstheater', in Sergej Tretjakow, *Ich will ein Kind haben. Zwei Fassungen. Materialien, Analysen, Meninungen*, ed. Eduard Ditschek (Berlin, forthcoming), pp. 272–99.
4. Mierau, *Erfindung und Korrektur*, p. 87. Fragments of the second version of *I Want a Child* were published in *Novyi Lef*, no. 3 (1927), pp. 3–11, and in *Nastoiashchee* (Novosibirsk), no. 3 (1929), pp. 20–1. The 1930 translation by Ernst Hube based on this version is reprinted in Mierau, *Erfindung und Korrektur*, pp. 179–246.
5. This fact is easily obscured by the historical experience of Nazi German eugenics and genocide that now separate us from the 1920s. The internal debates in the theatre censorship offices in 1928 (where Meyerhold was finally granted permission to stage *I Want a Child* as an exception to a general ban on the play) mainly concerned the question whether *a theatre* was the proper place to treat the subject; no one questioned the acceptability of an eugenic approach to parenthood as such. The minutes of the discussion in the theatre censorship Glavrepertkom are published in *Sovremennaia dramaturgiia*, 2 (1988), pp. 238–43.
6. Terentev's plan for his production was published in *Novyi Lef*, 12 (1928), pp. 32–5; Meyerhold's project is described in the minutes of the discussion in Glavrepertkom and in materials in TsGALI; German translation in Tretjakow, *Brülle, China! – Ich will ein Kind haben*, pp. 186–92. Lissitsky's

work on the setting, which went through at least five versions, is docu-
mented in Sophie Lissitzky-Kuppers (ed.), *El Lissitzky. Life, Letters, Texts*,
trans. Helene Aldwinckle and Mary Whittall (London, 1968), pp. 212–14.
For a detailed discussion of the two versions of the play and the production
projects, see Mierau, *Erfindung und Korrektur*, pp. 83–107, and 'Standard
auf der Bühne oder Fiasko dreier Meister', in his *Zwölf Arten die Welt zu
beschreiben* (Leipzig, 1988), pp. 100–8.

7.   One reason for the endless postponement of the production was allegedly
     that Lissitsky's sets could only be used in the projected Gropius-inspired
     building, which was not completed before Meyerhold's theatre was closed
     down in 1938. On the construction plans, see M. Barkhin and S. Vakhtangov,
     'Nezavershennyi zamysl'', in L. Vendrovskaia (ed.), *Vstrechi s
     Meierkhol'dom* (Moscow, 1967), pp. 570–8. Rudnitsky (*Russian and So-
     viet Theatre*, p. 198) remarks that after Meyerhold had managed to wrench
     the project out of the hands of the young pretender Terentev, he may have
     cooled toward the whole project.

8.   'Chto pishut dramaturgi. S. Tret'iakov', *Rabis*, 11 (1929), p. 7.

9.   Erwin Piscator, *Das politische Theater* (Rheinbek bei Hamburg, 1963), p.
     75.

10. *Brecht on Theatre*, pp. 33–42.

11. *Brecht on Theatre*, p. 60.

12. *Brecht on Theatre*, pp. 132–3.

13. *Brecht on Theatre*, p. 60.

14. Bertolt Brecht, *Gesammelte Werke*, vol. 15, p. 221.

15. See Mierau, *Erfindung und Korrektur*, p. 278.

16. Six months after first meeting Tretyakov, who was visiting Berlin in early
     1931, Brecht and his group began the film project *Kuhle Wampe*. The
     protagonist in one of the four episodes of the film is a young, strong and
     rational woman Communist who is expecting a child but is forced by her
     miserable social circumstances to have an abortion. The conflict between
     biology and society here seems to be the reverse of that in the first version
     of *I Want a Child*. The motif of the illegal abortion was to have been
     developed in the film, but the scenes were banned by the censor. See
     Wolfgang Gersch, *Film bei Brecht* (Berlin-DDR, 1975), pp. 99–139.

17. Much has been written in recent years on the Brecht–Tretyakov connection
     and on Brecht's other Soviet contacts. Detailed as they may be, these
     studies often suffer from a certain comparativist mania for constructing
     causal connections and correspondences from insufficiently interpreted
     facts. To take one small example that should merit at least a moment of
     second thought on the part of the comparativist, there is the fact that Brecht
     wrote the often-quoted poem 'Is the People Infallible?' after learning of
     Tretyakov's death in prison in 1939. But why did Brecht, who calls his
     dead friend 'mein lehrer', actually *cross out* the name 'tretjakow' follow-
     ing the word 'lehrer'(in the manuscript in the Brecht Archive, BBA 99/42–
     43)? What, after all, did Tretyakov teach? And what did Brecht learn?
     With no further ranking, the following are some noteworthy titles: Fritz
     Mierau, *Erfindung und Korrektur*; Marjorie Hoover, 'Brecht's Soviet Con-
     nection Tretiakov', *Brecht-Jahrbuch*, 3 (Frankfurt-am-Main, 1973), pp.
     39–56; Heinz Brüggeman, *Literarische Technik und soziale Revolution*

(Rheinbek bei Hamburg, 1973), pp. 139–164; Kathrine Bliss Eaton, *The Theater of Meyerhold and Brecht* (Westport, Conn., 1986), *passim*. My own attitude to the Brecht–Soviet connection is developed in *Stjärnfall*. The dialogue between Brecht and Eisenstein, set in 1932, is translated by Håkan Lövgren as 'In the Sign of Aquarius', in Kleberg and Lövgren (eds), *Eisenstein Revisited*, pp. 39–63; also in *Comparative Criticism*, vol. 14 (Cambridge, 1992), pp. 25–53.

Notes to Chapter 11

1. See Rudnitsky, *Russian and Soviet Theatre*, pp. 199–201.
2. S. Tret'iakov, 'Dramaturgovy zametki', *ZhI*, no. 46 (1927), p. 7.
3. Osip Brik, 'Ne v teatre, a v klube', *Lef*, no. 1 (5) (1924), p. 22.
4. Frantisek Déak, 'The Blue Blouses', *Drama Review*, 57 (1973), pp. 35–46. Even after he gave up playwriting for film and journalism, Tretyakov took great but not uncritical interest in the Blue Blouses and other new tendencies on the theatrical front. See his articles 'A dal'she?' *Siniaia bluza*, 3 (41) (1926), pp. 13–14; 'O "Sinei bluze"', *Al'bom Siniaia bluza SSSR* (Moscow, 1927), p. 6; and his speech at a public debate on the Blue Blouses, *Siniaia bluza*, 5 (77) (1928), pp. 60–1. Tretyakov was also one of the first critics to write favourably about the production of *The Government Inspector* by Igor Terentev, who planned to stage *I Want a Child*: 'Izobretatel'nyi teatr', *Rabochaia Moskva*, 24 May 1928, and 'Novatorstvo i filisterstvo', *Chitatel' i pisatel'*, 21 (1928), p. 5. Naturally, Tretyakov was the first to translate Brecht widely into Russian: B. Brekht, *Epicheskie dramy* (Moscow, 1934) contains his introduction and translations of *The Measures Taken*, *The Mother* and *Saint Joan of the Stockyards* (none of which were ever staged). His plans to write new plays, possibly together with Hans Eisler or even with Brecht, however, remained unrealised; see Mierau, *Erfindung und Korrektur*, *passim*.
5. For an overview of the years 1925–30, see Rudnitsky, *Russian and Soviet Theatre*, ch. 4, 'Extremes Converge', pp. 185–264.
6. Tairov, *Notes of a Director*, p. 143.
7. An outstanding analysis of this classic and enigmatic production is in Picon-Vallin, *Meyerhold*, pp. 264–339. For our discussion, one background text for Meyerhold's work is of immediate relevance. The director specially commissioned an essay by the erudite Vyacheslav Ivanov (who at the time had emigrated to Italy) on the ancient theatre and the pre-Aristophanean comedy, where the cleansing of the sins of the collective (in the so-called *parabasis*) plays a key role. Ivanov's essay, '"Revizor" Gogolia i komediia Aristofana', was published by Meyerhold in his theatre's miscellany *Teatral'nyi Oktiabr'*, 1 (Moscow–Leningrad, 1926), pp. 89–99; an English translation of this fascinating text is published as 'Gogol's *Inspector General* and the Comedy of Aristophanes', in Robert A. Maguire (ed.), *Gogol from the Twentieth Century: Eleven Essays* (Princeton, 1974), pp. 199–215.
8. The 'parodical' aspect of the discourse of the 1930s is demonstrated in my

discussion about Mei Lan-fang's theatre, 'The Sorcerer's Apprentices';
see chapter 8, note 14 above.

Notes to Postscript

1. The exhibition catalogue *Paris–Moscou 1900–1930* (Paris, 1979) provides
    a magnificent but unclearly structured textual and pictorial survey of the
    period. As is especially clear in the commentaries, the joint French-Soviet
    arrangers obviously tried to find a 'middle road' between the established
    Soviet and Western views on the material. Critical views of the exhibition
    presented by Russian émigrés and French observers of the Soviet Union
    are collected in *Culture et pouvoir communiste. L'autre face de 'Paris–
    Moscou'*, a special issue of the journal *Recherches* (no. 39, October 1979).
    Reflecting the impact of Solzhenitsyn's *The Gulag Archipelago* (translated
    in the West, beginning in 1974) and the lively French reaction to it, the
    publication contains perhaps the first attempts to revise the dualistic view
    of the relationship between the avant-garde and the culture of the Stalin
    period.
2. Boris Groys, *Gesamtkunstwerk Stalin. Die gespaltene Kultur in der
    Sowjetunion*, trans. by Gabriele Leupold (Munich, 1988), p. 42.
3. Groys, *Gesamtkunstwerk Stalin*, p. 19.
4. Groys, *Gesamtkunstwerk Stalin*, pp. 11–12, 26–7, 36–7.
5. Groys, *Gesamtkunstwerk Stalin*, pp. 24, 33.
6. Boris Groys, 'The Birth of Socialist Realism from the Spirit of the Russian
    Avant-Garde', in Hans Günther (ed.), *The Culture of the Stalin Period*
    (London, 1990), p. 125.
7. Groys, *Gesamtkunstwerk Stalin*, p. 81.
8. The constructivist avant-garde was predominantly a Moscow phenom-
    enon. An entire paradigm could even be proposed for the 1920s and 1930s:

LENINGRAD	MOSCOW
time	*space*
acmeism	futurism
Mandelstam	Mayakovsky
Akhmatova	Pasternak
poetry	*theatre*
formalists:	sociologists:
Tynianov/Eikhenbaum	Brik/Arvatov
Filonov	Tatlin
OBERIU	constructivism
Zoshchenko	Pilnyak
Shostakovich	Prokofiev
Bakhtin	Eisenstein
context	*text*

In this paradigm, seemingly private travel (between the two capitals or
elsewhere) might acquire new significance. Consider also important shifts
such as Meyerhold's moving from Petrograd to Moscow (via Novorosiisk)
to lead the 'October Revolution in the Theatre' in 1920, or Malevich's

departure from Moscow in 1919 to start his own school, UNOVIS, in Vitebsk, moving on in 1921 to Petrograd to teach at the InKhuk there. I owe the idea and some of the pairs of the paradigm (although not the Leningrad–Moscow axis) to a lecture by Peter Alberg Jensen at Stockholm University.

9. Groys, *Gesamtkunstwerk Stalin*, p. 130.
10. A still valuable study on the 'proletarian' realists (whose background, as a rule, was provincial Red Army rather than working class) is Edward J. Brown, *The Proletarian Episode in Russian Literature: 1928–1932* (New York, 1953). See also Miroslav Drozda and Milan Hrala, *Dvacátá léta*; Hans Günther, *Die Verstaatlichung der Literatur* (Stuttgart, 1984); and the contributions by Aleksandr Flaker and Boris Groys to Günther (ed.), *The Culture of the Stalin Period.*
11. The avant-garde did not have far to turn for a model of undoctrinaire thinking: it was to be found in the formalist critic Yury Tynianov's concept of structural function as presented in the essays 'The Literary Fact' and 'On Literary Evolution', the first of which, in fact, appeared in the avant-garde's own journal *Lef*, no. 2 (1924). Tynianov's second essay is translated in Ladislav Matejka and Krystyna Pomorska (eds), *Readings in Russian Poetics. Formalist and Structuralist Views* (Ann Arbor, 1978), pp. 66–78.
12. Lars Kleberg, *Teatern som handling. Sovjetisk avantgardeestetik 1917–1927*, second edn (Stockholm, 1980), p. 146.
13. Groys, 'The Birth of Socialist Realism from the Spirit of the Avant-Garde', p. 146. Cf. also p. 145 on the 'engineers of the human soul':

> The real difference between the avant-garde and Socialist Realism consists . . . in moving the centre of gravity from work on the basis to work on the superstructure (avant-garde work on the superstructure being assumed by Stalin), which was expressed in the first instance in projecting the New Man as an element of the new reality rather than in merely projecting its purely technical, material aspects.

14. The word 'only' should not be understood as diminishing the weight of Tretyakov's extremism. One unusually brutal text of his is the address he delivered on the occasion of the tenth anniversary of the State Publishing House in 1929, entitled 'the Brain-Processing Factory'. There he exhorts the celebrator to 'liquidate the privileges of the artistic sector and integrate it into other normal branches of publishing'. By so doing, he concludes, the Publishing House will become what it ought to be, 'a planified brain-processing factory in the socialist economy' (*Pisateli Gosizdatu 1919–1929* [Moscow and Leningrad, 1929] p. 86). This sounds like 'engineers of the human soul' ahead of the fact, although the difference between 'brain' and 'soul' is nevertheless worth noting. Tretyakov's earlier article 'Standard' can only compare with Alexei Gastev in its pedantic proposals for the 'rationalisation' of everyday life, in this case that of the members of the Proletkult Workers' Theatre ('Standart', *Oktiabr' mysli*, no. 2 (1924), pp. 30–3). 'Standard' could well have been the butt of Zamyatin's mockery in the parodical anti-utopian novel *We* (1920), had it not been written four years *later*.

   The concept of parody in the relationship between the avant-garde and

Socialist Realism may deserve further reflection. In the quotation from the earlier version of the present study (note 12 above), I used the expression 'grim parody' for the Stalinist transposition of the avant-garde's technicism into the ideological sphere. However, many 'maximalist' statements can in themselves sound unintentionally parodical (as Zamyatin's sensitive ear detected immediately). The Stalinist utilisation of these notions, which had fatal consequences for their maximalist authors as well, could thus be interpreted as a 'parody of the parody' ('negation of the negation'), or 'meta-tragedy'. In the same way, the avant-garde's imitation of the political field sometimes came close to masquerade (in language, behaviour, clothing, and so on; my book provides some material for such an interpretation). Stalinism would in this sense mean the transformation of the leftist avant-gardists' everyday 'theatre' into irrevocable 'action'.

15.   Most notably in the introduction to the first comprehensive history of the period, *Istoriia sovetskogo teatra*, part 1 [never continued] (Leningrad, 1933), pp. xi–xxvii which in fact denounced the entire book for its uncritical attitude to the proto-fascist ideas of Wagner and Nietzsche and their Russian followers. Persons under attack such as Lunacharsky and Adrian Piotrovsky, theoretician of the mass spectacle, were forced to revise their Wagnerism without, however, totally giving in to the new line. See their contributions to the brochure *Malyi Opernyi Teatr – Rikhard Vagner* (Leningrad, 1933), pp. 3–5 and 7–8, and A. Piotrovskii, 'Teatral'noe delo Vagnera', *Rabochii teatr*, no. 3–4 (1933), pp. 5–6. Soon the name of Wagner was exorcised from Soviet theatre ideology, although his basic contribution was retained. During the Nazi German-Soviet Pact (1939–41) Wagner was temporarily rehabilitated, notably in Eisenstein's staging of *Die Walküre* at the Bolshoi Theatre in 1940; see my imagined dialogue between Eisenstein and Bakhtin, 'Ash Wednesday', in *Stjärnfall*, pp. 77–110; French trans. in *La chute des étoiles*, pp. 89–137.

16.   See Alexander Fevral'skii, *Zapiski rovesnika veka* (Moscow, 1976), pp. 306–7.

Biographical Notes

Arvatov, Boris (1896–1940). Literary and art critic. After the Civil War active in the Moscow Proletkult, where he defended futurism and avant-garde art. During the 1920s one of the most radical spokesmen of the theory of production art.

Bogdanov, Alexander (1873–1928). Socialist philosopher, author of the general organisation theory, 'tectology'. A leading Bolshevik until 1908, then opponent to political work inside the existing legal institutions. Ideological founder of the Proletkult movement.

Brik, Osip (1888–1945). Literary critic, one of the leading Russian formalists. After the Revolution spokesman of production art, close collaborator of Mayakovsky, co-editor of the journals *Lef* (1923–5) and *New Lef* (1927–8).

Eisenstein, Sergey (1898–1948). Director at the Moscow Proletkult Theatre 1920–4, later leading director, theorist and pedagogue of the Soviet cinema.

Ivanov, Vyacheslav (1866–1949). Symbolist poet and philosopher, erudite Greek philologist, arguing for the revival of the connection between art and cult. Emigrated to Italy in 1924.

Kerzhentsev, Platon (1881–1940). Critic, cultural politician. Prominent Proletkult leader, later a diplomat and journalist.

Lunacharsky, Anatoly (1875–1933). Marxist literary critic, cultural politician. People's Commissar of Enlightenment 1917–29.

Malevich, Kazimir (1878–1935). Painter and art theorist, 'suprematist'. Author of the famous *Black Square* (1913) and, in the 1920s, of three-dimensional non-figurative compositions.

Mayakovsky, Vladimir (1893–1930).   Poet, playwright. The most prominent futurist poet – lyrical, satirical and agitational. A central figure in the 'left art' movement of the 1920s, founder of the journals *Lef* and *New Lef*. Committed suicide.

Meyerhold, Vsevolod (1874–1940).   Actor and theatre director. Started out as a student of Stanislavsky, from 1905 anti-naturalist theatrical reformer. After the Revolution theatre politician, author of the biomechanical system of acting, head of the State Meyerhold Theatre (TIM) 1922–38. Arrested in 1939, executed.

Tairov, Alexander (1885–1950).   Actor and theatre director. Founder and head of the Kamerny Theatre in Moscow 1914–50.

Tatlin, Vladimir (1885–1953).   Painter, author of three-dimensional non-figurative objects, after the Revolution of the constructivist *Monument to the Third International* and the experimental aeroplane, 'Letatlin'.

Tretyakov, Sergey (1892–1939).   Poet, playwright, reporter. Left-wing futurist, during the late 1920s spokesman of the 'literature of fact'. Arrested in 1937, died in prison.

Yevreinov, Nikolay (1879–1953).   Playwright, director, theatre theorist. Explorer of 'theatricalism' and the 'theatrical instinct'. Emigrated in 1925.

Index